The Brain has a
Mind of its Own

For Alice, Asher and Alexander

Jeremy Holmes

The Brain has a Mind of its Own

Attachment, Neurobiology, and the New Science of Psychotherapy

CONFER
BOOKS

Published in 2020 by Confer Books, London

www.confer.uk.com

Registered office:
21 California, Martlesham, Woodbridge, Suffolk IP12 4DE, England

5 7 9 10 8 6 4

This is a work of nonfiction. Any similarity between the characters and situations
within its pages, and places, persons, or animals living or dead, could be
unintentional and co-incidental. Some names and identifying details have been
changed or omitted to, in part, protect the privacy of individuals.

British Library Cataloguing in Publication Data. A catalogue record for this book is
available from the British Library.

ISBN: 978-1-913494-02-5 (paperback)
ISBN: 978-1-913494-03-2 (ebook)

Typeset by Bespoke Publishing Ltd.
Printed in the UK by Ashford Colour Press

Contents

INTRODUCTION

Freud's most creative years, as he moved from the seeming certainties of pre-twentieth-century science to the modernistic project of psychoanalysis, paralleled and pioneered the cultural shifts of the new century. Our millennium has seen a return to a mechanistic study of the mind, based on brain imaging and artificial intelligence. My aim in this book is to explore the implications of this neuroscience revolution for psychotherapy, and to argue that psychoanalysis still has much to contribute to our understanding of what it is to be human. What I'm attempting should be thought of as an *essay* – in the sense of effort or trial – encapsulating a personal angle on a topic.

We now know beyond doubt that psychoanalytic psychotherapy produces significant and sustained psychological changes for people suffering from psychological distress (e.g., Leichsenring, 2008; Shedler, 2010; Taylor, 2015).

But the underlying *mechanisms* – what it is about therapists, patients, and their co-created therapy which produces change – remain mysterious (Wampold, 2015). There is no shortage of theories: the therapeutic alliance, empathy, mutative interpretations, cognitive restructuring, restoration of family hierarchy and communication channels, unconditional positive regard. The answers probably include all of the above, and more. But, for many reasons, including the difficulty of meaningfully fitting psychotherapy into a randomised controlled trial paradigm, and "allegiance effects" (Kim, Wampold, & Bolt, 2004), where researcher's bias – or transference – unconsciously affects their findings, however much they strive to counteract this, the evidence remains equivocal.

The processes implicated in psychotherapy are multiple: the psychotherapist herself, her personality and skill, the character and motivation of the patient, the nature and severity of the illness, the model, duration, and frequency of treatment, and the social context within which therapy is practised. Given this complexity, linear explanations – if therapists do or say this, then that improvement will result – are unlikely to account for the phenomena (Masterpaqua & Perna, 1997). The famous "dodo bird verdict" (Budd & Hughes, 2009), "All have won and everyone shall have prizes", and the integrative meta-model perspective it implies, still holds firm. But complacency is contraindicated: although therapy undoubtedly can do good, it does not succeed in all cases – around 50–60 per cent of patients improve, 10 per cent deteriorate, while at least 30 per cent remain roughly where they were when they started (Lambert, 2013). For publicly funded therapies, allocating resources to ineffective treatment is wasteful, and for therapists it gives their beloved discipline a bad name.

The situation is not unlike that faced by Darwin when he published *On the Origin of Species* in 1856 (Holmes & Slade, 2017, 2019).

Using qualitative evidence from the fossil, geological, and his own and Wallace's observational record, he intuited how species adapt and evolve by natural selection. But Darwin's knowledge of inheritance went no further than the folk understanding that offspring both resemble and differ from their parents. Pre-Mendel, pre-Huxley, pre-Watson & Crick, pre-CRISPR, he was entirely ignorant of the genetic mechanisms involved. Psychotherapy is similarly in the dark about its own "DNA". This book's project is to argue that advances in neuroscience point to new understandings of how psychotherapy produces psychic change.

My starting point is a new paradigm, the *Free Energy Principle* (FEP), which has swept through academic psychology and brain research but which, a few pioneers excepted (e.g., Connolly, 2018; Hopkins, 2016; Mellor, 2018; Moutoussis, Shahar, Hauser, & Dolan, 2018; Smith, Lane, Nadel, & Moutoussis, 2019a; Smith, Lane, Parr, & Friston, 2019b; Solms, 2019), has had little impact within the world of psychotherapy. I will gradually try to unfold the full nature and psychotherapeutic implications of FEP, but start with a summary of its main contours. Key concepts are italicised.

Energy in FEP is not a physical phenomenon like heat, or electromagnetic radiation, but a superordinate explanatory category, akin to gravity (cf. Connolly & van Deventer, 2017), with both mental and physical connotations. FEP is a *principle* or framework for understanding the fundamentals of psychic life, conscious and unconscious, analogous, and not unrelated to, Freud's pleasure and reality principles.

According to the FEP, the brain's task is to select from, attend to, shape, and *maintain homeostasis* in the face of the streams of incoming neural energy from both its sense organs and its *interoceptive* and proprioceptive internal milieu. It does this by *predicting*, "top-down", on the basis of previous experience, the likely meanings of this "bottom-up" input. These predictions follow the mathematics of the eighteenth-century cleric Thomas Bayes, and are thus known as "*Bayesian*". The ever-changing discrepancies between prediction and sensation, between our *generative models* of the world and reality, activate *Prediction Error Minimisation* (PEM), in which the brain "instructs" itself to modify *prior* models of the world in the light of experience, whereby they become *posteriors*, and take *actions* which improve precision, *clarify ambiguity*, and align input with expectations.

From a psychotherapeutic viewpoint, interoceptions (i.e., bodily feelings) are especially important because they underpin *affective life*. In general, prediction errors – the discrepancies between what we want/expect and what our senses tell us is the case – are experienced as "bad" or painful, thereby motivating their minimisation. Conversely, when expectation and experience align, we feel "good" or happy. The psychological distress that brings people for psychotherapeutic help can be conceived as chronic states of unresolved prediction error. The aim of psychotherapy is to redress these by mobilising the capacity for action and model revision.

In FEP, energy is either *free*, or *bound*. Free energy reflects the ever-changing and potentially chaotic nature of the impact of the environment on the physical, psychological, and interpersonal self. Energy's role is therefore *ambiguous*: it provides the vital information and sustenance needed for our evolutionarily derived tasks of adaptation, survival, and reproduction, and arguably forms the basis for creativity, but, unbound, can overwhelm the unprepared nervous system. The need to find and bind free energy is what motivates us, what "makes us tick", what makes us exploit what we have, and explore and want to know more, and to think up better world models; failure to do so is demotivating, degenerating, and depressing.

All this has psychoanalytic resonances. Freud first proposed an interplay between free and bound energy (or Q as he symbolised it) within the mind/brain in his abandoned and un-published "project" (Carhart-Harris & Friston, 2010; Freud, 1950a) which he titled "psychology for neurologists". As psychoanalysis evolved, the Q-concept transmuted into *libido*. Through ca-thexis, or *binding*, libido invests its objects with desire, leading in the short or long run to pleasur-able discharge (Freud, 1911b, 1920g). In Freud's schema, energy/libido unbound, especially in the shape of *incestuous* desire, has to be held at bay by primal repression (Barratt, 2019), whose lurking untamed presence makes the human subject inherently vulnerable to neurosis.

The FEP and Bayesian model are the brain-children of Karl Friston (2010) and his many colleagues (e.g., Clark, 2016; Hohwy, 2013; Hopkins, 2016). Note that "Fristianity" is pri-marily a statistical and mathematical schema. Thanks (or, rather, unthanks) to my mathe-matical limitations, this exposition is entirely prose-bound, a constraint which critics might legitimately compare with trying to make sense of cosmology or quantum physics without using equations (it can be done, see Rovelli, 2017).

The plan of the book follows. Chapter 1 lays out the intellectual origins and current state of FEP. For the PEM uninitiated this first chapter may be hard going, but be reassured: Chapter 2 shows how the apparently abstract and cognitive slant of FEP resonates with everyday experience, and with psychoanalytic thinking. Chapter 3 brings in the role of attachment, and in our hyper-social species, how PEM is typically done collaboratively, but how insecure forms of attachment can jeopardise this, so exposing potential sufferers to failure of PEM, or energy unbound. Chapter 4 uses an FEP perspective to look at the kinds of difficulties and diagnoses which bring people for psychotherapeutic help. Chapter 5 takes the specific procedures of psychoanalytic work – dream interpretation, free association, and the ambiguities of transference – and shows how they uncouple top-down from bottom-up automaticity, enabling scrutiny of why and where

PEM is problematic. Based on FEP, Chapters 6 and 7 discuss therapist–client attachments, the conversations they engender, and how they can help unravel stuck PEM procedures. Chapter 8 summarises the implications of FEP for psychotherapeutic work in the real world of the consulting room. I conclude with a brief glossary of FEP-related terms which I hope will help readers new to this novel conceptual universe.

In addition to acknowledging maths-deficit, a few other caveats are needed. I shall say much about "conversation" between top-down representations and bottom-up sensations, and the role of language as a mediator between them. This hierarchy reveals how language structures thought, implying dominance/submission, while the thrust of the essay is a plea for the health-giving properties of more equal, "democratic" interchange between the sensual and the representational (cf. Bollas, 2019).

I have also felt free to select between cultural givens. Thus: in equipoise, the feminine pronoun is preferred; the terms client and patient are used interchangeably; psychotherapy is sometimes meant in a generic sense, but usually to refer to its psychoanalytic varieties. Finally, having worked daily with psychological pain, delusion, and confusion, I endorse Hopson's (2019) aperçu that, had King Lear, sensing incipient dementia, cried out "*Oh let me not suffer from mental health issues, sweet heaven*" a vital, if painful, truth would have been lost!

The Free Energy Principle

Gabbard and Ogden (2009), perhaps unconsciously echoing *Totem and Taboo* (Freud, 1912–13), describe the paradoxical post-qualification trajectory for members of the psychoanalytic clan as having both to "kill the father" and to "honour one's ancestors". In that spirit, my exposition of FEP is part homage to Freud, part search for a post-psychoanalytic paradigm. Newton famously acknowledged, *"If I have seen further it is because I have stood on the shoulders of giants."* Before describing FEP, I honour the progenitors whose ideas form the background to our story.

FIVE FOUNDING FATHERS

Contemporary neuroscience starts from the work of Hermann von Helmholtz (1821–1894), polymath, physician, physicist, proponent of the conservation of energy, pioneer of the ophthalmoscope, and tutor to Freud's mentor, Ernst Brucke (Bernfeld, 1944; Dayan, Hinton, Neal, & Zemel, 1995). Three of Helmholtz's ideas are especially relevant to our discussion. First, much as Helmholtz admired Goethe as a poet, he and his group rejected soulful romanticism in favour of the scientific method and, when it came to the brain/ mind, to a strictly monistic materialistic outlook.

Helmholtz saw the brain as a hierarchical "inference machine" (Badcock, Friston, Maxwell, & Ramstead, 2019) in which bottom-up sensations (initially from sensory epithelia) are appraised and interact with top-down cortex-derived constructs and meanings. This hierarchical model also applies to "all stations between", meaning intermediate levels of brain function in which the activity of modulatory neurons is continuously adjusted in the light of impulses from both above and below.

Helmholtz's constructivism is especially important, as his ideas contrast with the still widely held model in which sense organs are thought of as transmitting a one-way, camera-like "representation" of "reality" to a passive receiving brain. By contrast, the Helmholtzian mind *makes its own world* in a dynamic fashion, constantly updating its models in the light of experience. The phenomenological "reality" which we experience is a *virtual reality* projected onto the theatre of the mind (cf. Humphrey, 2011).

Helmholtz also proposed that much of mental life goes on below conscious awareness. Freud's conscious/unconscious and ego/id/superego meta-psychologies were constructed from Helmholtzian building blocks.

Our second forefather is familiar to all high-school students of biology. Claude Bernard (1813–1878) pioneered the use of scientific methods in medicine, including blinded controlled trials. His famous assertion that "*the stability of the interior milieu is the condition of a free life*" introduced the concept of homeostasis into biology. Although applicable primarily to physiological phenomena such as temperature regulation, his ideas about physiological homeostasis can be extended to the workings of the brain/mind.

Homeostasis is now seen as part of the more general phenomenon of *allostasis*. Living in an ever-evolving environment, like Heraclitus's river, we stay the same by continuously changing. We keep cool in hot weather not just by sweating and peripheral vasodilatation, but by moving into shade, shedding clothes, switching on fans, etc. Comparably, at an interpersonal level we maintain stability – in psychopathology maladaptive stability – by allostatically choosing or shaping our relational milieu so that it resembles conditions which resonate with past experience (psychoanalytically through "projective identification"). Allostasis is relevant to the adverse consequences of childhood trauma, in which the body's physiological attempts to maintain stability, for example by activation of the HPA axis, if prolonged, can have negative consequences: hyperactivation of the immune system, psychological over-arousal, etc. (Caspi et al., 2002). As we shall see, PEM is essentially a homeostatic enterprise in which the mind/brain registers and then tries to minimise deviations from its desired states (Barrett, 2017; Solms, 2019).

Homeostasis takes us to our next hero, Freud (1856–1939) himself, and his "principle of constancy":

> *[T]he purpose of the mental apparatus [is]*
> *to keep as low as possible the total amount*
> *of the excitations to which it is subject.*
> *(1925d, p. 3)*

Freud's early (1895) speculations about neural energy and its "occupation" or cathexis (1950a) became the psychological concepts of libido, bound and unbound (1911b, 1920g). He held fast to this fundamental distinction to the end of his life:

> *We seem to recognize that nervous or psy-*
> *chical energy occurs in two forms, one freely*
> *mobile and another, by comparison, bound.*
> *(1940a, p. 141)*

He conceived the primary processes of "unbound energy" in quantitative terms, in which psychic energy is "slowed down" sufficiently for thought, as opposed to "discharge" in the form of action or symptomatology. For thinking to occur, "the conversion of freely displaceable cathexes into 'bound' cathexes was necessary" (Freud, 1911b, p. 303; see Holt, 1962). Bound energy is characteristic of secondary processes, encompassing language, ego-mediated restraint, and superego prohibitions.

In FEP terms, Freud's primary processes are bottom-up impulses emanating from sensory epithelia together with interoceptions, stimulating and interacting with the top-down secondary processes of affective modulation, verbal representations, and logic (Northoff & Panksepp, 2008). Also relevant is Freud's emphasis on traumatic memories, which, unmodulated and regulated, remain disruptively unbound.

Laplanche & Pontalis (1973, p. 52), with their francophone linguistic sensibility, link energy *binding* with *bound*aries, or the capacity to hold something in place rather than giving free rein to its ambiguous creative/destructive potential. This takes us to our next intellectual giant, Erwin Schroedinger (1887–1961), Nobel prize-winning quantum physicist, who was also interested in biology.

Posing the question *"What is life?"*, Schroedinger's answer was "negative entropy" (1944) or *negentropy* (Ramstead, Badcock, & Friston, 2017). The second law of thermodynamics holds that the universe tends irreversibly towards disorder, that is, entropy. The cup of tea or coffee which you, dear reader, are perhaps currently drinking, will, if left to itself while you attend to a pressing chore, inexorably become cooler with the passage of time – never hotter! Its energy, and the "order" (i.e., directed heat) introduced in its making, will have dissipated into the surroundings, slightly raising the temperature of the surroundings. Contrast this with living entities – an amoeba, tree, or a human being. Life, in contrast to cups of coffee, maintains its order and structure over time, and so manifests *negative* entropy, or *negentropy*, as opposed to disorder and dissolution. The semi-permeable boundaries and metabolic processes of living beings ensure that order rules. Disorder is expelled/excreted into the entropic surroundings, in contrast to living entities – but only during their "lifetime".

Bernard's homeostasis represents the efforts needed to maintain living processes in the face of the onslaughts of surrounding entropy. Returning to Freud (1940a), still faithful to his unpublished project, he makes a similar point in his contrast between the life and death instincts:

[T]he aim [of Eros] is to establish even greater unities and to preserve them thus – in short, to bind together; *the aim of [Thanatos] is, on the contrary to* undo connections *and so to destroy things. (p. 148, my emphasis)*

Death represents irreversible dissolution, that is, unbinding, of boundaries. The "death instinct" represents the inexorable victory of entropy over negentropy. From a psychoanalytic perspective, Barratt (2019) sees this balance between eros and "deathfulness" not so much as representing aggression or the static categories of conventional psychoanalysis – id, ego, etc. – but rather as reflecting the fluidity and flux of existence. From an FEP perspective, there is a never fully resolved dynamic interchange or "conversation" between the bottom-up impact of the entropic external world – including one's negentropic fellow humans – and top-down attempts to bind free energy, and so enhance adaptation and survival.

This leads to our fifth, and chronologically preceding presiding genius, the Reverend Thomas Bayes (1702–1761). Bayes was one of the founders of probability theory. His "theorum" has had implications far beyond the realm of statistics. Bayes-ism has been described as "maths on top of common sense" (Devlin, 2003). The "common sense" version goes as follows. We live in an uncertain universe. We cannot know the future, yet if we are to adapt – and ultimately survive and reproduce – we need to unravel the meaning of what our sense organs tell us and make *good guesses* about "what is going on" now and what's likely to happen in the future. We need to know who and what to trust; what is nutritious and what poisonous; to lie down with the lamb but not the lion; when to wield the pen, when the sword. That's the brain's purpose. But, inevitably, it gets things wrong, in lesser or greater ways. As we shall see, the job of psychotherapy is repair, or "re-minding", in all its senses.

KARL FRISTON AND "FREE ENERGY"

Let's move now from these precursors to contemporary neuroscience. Here too there is a magisterial figure, Karl Friston, a mathematical neuroscientist and psychiatrist, whose ideas form the substrate for much of what follows (Friston, 2010; Hobson & Friston, 2012; Friston & Frith, 2015). Friston's model can be broken down into a number of key propositions.

STABLE SYSTEMS NEED TO SAMPLE THEIR ENVIRONMENT FOR RELEVANT INFORMATION

Information about the surrounding environment is essential to an organism's survival – availability of foodstuffs, whereabouts of potential mates, predators, etc. But information-gathering is selective – we only need to know what we need to know. Sensory systems work within a range bounded on each side by the familiar and the alien. Aquatic creatures take their watery realm for granted, but a fish out of water triggers full piscean alarm. These are its "*affordances*", what its environment offers, provides, or furnishes to the individual, for good or ill (Gibson, 1986). Depending on its environmental niche, each species' brain is evolutionarily designed to select *salient* features from its environment and ignore those that are irrelevant. The mind/brain needs to compute both *precision* (to what extent its prior models of the world correspond with sensory input), but also the overall meaning or *context* of its input, within time frames that get longer and longer as we ascend the neuronal hierarchy towards consciousness.

The concept of *attention* captures the capacity to concentrate on relevant stimuli and ignore the irrelevant (Ramstead, Veissiere, & Kirmayer, 2016). We are especially attuned to notice *anomalies*. Psychotherapists are good at this: for instance, a client who fails to mention her father when describing her childhood, or consistently uses an ironic mocking tone while describing her husband. These anomalies, of which the client may be unaware, point to unconscious themes freighted with significance, usually of avoided emotional pain, which the therapist will invite the client jointly to consider. We shall see later how free association captures the minutiae of the "present moment" (cf. Yalom, 2011), which, if encompassed with a trusted companion, enhances the coherence of our experiential universe.

NEURAL SYSTEMS PERFORM ACTIVE INFERENCE (AI) TO MINIMISE UNCERTAINTY/SURPRISE

The brain eschews uncertainty and surprise, and gets an affective payoff from actively reducing both. A surprising sensory input is simply one that is unlikely, that is, has low probability, in the light of what we expect. Mathematically, surprise can be measured by the negative log-probability of sensory data, given our model of the world, which is higher the closer to zero is the probability. If something is totally improbable, it is totally surprising.

Probability curves the shapes we use to think with. Consider what's involved in catching a thrown ball, or a dog chasing a stick. Given a state of affairs A, where the ball is now, what I know about the power of the thrower's arm, the weight of the ball, and the pull of gravity, my curve prediction tells me that it will have reached point B in X milliseconds, so I move myself and my hands correspondingly. Given the relative speeds of neurotransmission and the ball's flight I'll need to adjust my prediction's precision if I am to get into the right place at the right time. I'll need to know where I am in space-time, as well as the ball, and thus a degree of "self-knowledge" (which may be of the most primitive kind) is needed for all motile life – all animals.

The brain uses "quick and dirty" methods to work fast. There is always a degree of error, due to noise in the circuits, and the limitations of time. *Active inference* implies rough integration methods to calculate areas under approximate curves, and rapidly applying these predictions to fill in the gaps, based on likely probabilities. Predictions are then optimised by comparison with real-world data, aiming all the time to eliminate as far as possible any remaining surprise. If the "ball" turns out to be a soap bubble, we revise our predictions and seek confirmatory evidence, for example, the ephemerality and iridescence which we'd expect with the latter but not the former.

Moving to longer timescales, Bayes still applies. The past is our only guide to the future: we make "*prior*" predictions based on previous experience. We need to know how much *error* is built into those "priors", how *precise* they are, or can be. Since the sun has never been known not to rise in the east we can discount the chances of a west-rising dawn, and turn our *attention* – whose function Freud (1911b, p. 302) from an FEP perspective presciently defined as meeting "the sense-impressions half-way, instead of [passively] awaiting their appearance" – perhaps to early morning beauty and the sounds of larks.

But when it comes to fellow humans, things are far less certain. A baby crying for his mother will find that there will be times when she comes at once; at others she is inexplicably delayed. In order to make predictions about people, we need to go quite high up the inferential hierarchy, to work out "what's going on" or *mentalise*: "Maybe she's tired, angry with me, intoxicated, making a new baby with Dad". In the interpersonal world, the Bayesian brain's task is to actively infer causes, affects, motivations, and meanings.

For two main reasons there will always be discrepancies between these top-down inferences, and what reality affords us. First, because the environment, human and physical, never stays still: by today, yesterday's priors will already be out of date. Second, because our sense organs are inherently fallible: they provide only a sample of all possible information, and these sampling capacities are in themselves imperfect. The discrepancies between bottom-up input and top-down inference, or "*prediction error*" needs to be built into our calculations, and then, as best we can, *minimised* (PEM). And to do so, we need to know how much *weight* to put on our sensory information and prior predictions.

BRAINS CREATE THEIR OWN WORLDS, INNER AND OUTER

With the "cognitive revolution" (Pinker, 2003) the predominant psychology paradigm reverted from black-box behaviourism to a "cognitive" model, in which the external world is "represented" in the mind. But, as we've seen, in the PEM third wave, the brain no longer merely "represents" the world, but *creates its own world*. Following Nagel's famous paper (1974), the "world" as we experience it, no less than that of a bat, is as much a product of our species' affordances as it is of an irreducible "reality". We "are" the air we breathe, the food we eat, the energy we absorb, and the self-organising, self-evolving, self-aware, "auto-poetic" (Kirchhoff, 2017) systems these have generated. At the higher reaches of the neural hierarchy – that is, self-aware-ness – these confirm to us what it is that we are: "Ah, that's me, my family, my house, my breakfast, my football team", etc. As we shall see, in an inherently uncertain world, the self has two complementary strategies: through *action/agency*, to seek out and shape the world in its own image, and/or continuously to *revise its generative models* of the world in which it finds itself.

LIVING ORGANISMS ARE BOUNDED

Mammalian brains are bounded within skulls (unlike those of cephalopods located in their tentacles). Everything we know about our environment – external and internal – derives ultimately from our sensory epithelia. We know no more about the world than what our sense organs tell us, have told us in the past, and the meanings and models we have built from this information.

This interface or boundary between bottom-up sensation and top-down model is known as a Markov blanket, named after the Russian mathematician Markov, 1856–1922. A Markov blanket is an artificial intelligence concept, in which incoming information and top-down models of the world are determined only by their inward and outward directions of travel, and cannot directly "speak" to one another.

This "blanket" metaphor reminds us that inherent uncertainty ("noise") afflicts both sensory input (precision – our sense organs "get things wrong") and models of the world (complexity – we get the "wrong end of sticks"); there is a limit to the completeness of our knowledge of the world, leading to epistemological doubt at every level (cf. Hopkins, 2016). Organisms need to find ways of living with, and overcoming this uncertainty. In the world of psychotherapy, being able to tolerate "not knowing" is a cardinal virtue.

Markov blankets characterise the environment/sensory epithelia interface, but also the different levels of the nervous system's hierarchy of upflowing sensory information and top-down interpretation of these signals. Although ultimately neuronal, these Markov blanket interfaces can be thought of as statistical, probabilistic boundaries. The different levels of the brain function as a "council of experts", balancing the information from the sense organs against predictions arising in higher brain regions. The degree to which a prediction error will be expressed (and experienced) depends upon its *precision*. This means our "council" also has to estimate the likely error of its errors – that is, how probable it is to be "right". We shall see how the FEP viewpoint suggests that "mis-settings" of these estimates can lead to the kinds of psychopathology which drives people to seek psychotherapeutic help.

ENERGY IS INFORMATIONAL AS WELL AS NEURO-ELECTRICAL

Claude Shannon, another seminal FEP figure, was working at the Bell telephone laboratories in the 1950s. He was interested in "data transfer", or how telephone interlocutors communicate across distance and how their words are translated into and out of electrical pulses. He studied strings of letters, noticing that the rarer the event, the greater its *informational content*. (In the crossword game Scrabble, the letter Z is 'worth' 10x more than an E.) Shannon's breakthrough was to realise that thermodynamic entropy equations could also be applied to information. Maximum entropy is where there is no information, such as an entirely fuzzy TV screen, or an indecipherable telephone message. Negentropy – that is, structure and order – is high in information in this technical sense.

Shannon saw that probability could be recast as *surprise* – the less probable an event, the more surprising it is, and vice versa. Friston's breakthrough was to realise that Shannon's equations for informational uncertainty (aka surprise), entropy, and "free energy", could, and indeed *must*, equally apply to the brain.

BRAIN AS A "HELMHOLTZ MACHINE"

We are now in a position to assemble the Friston model of the brain as a "*Helmholtz machine*" (Dayan, Hinton, Neal, & Zemel, 1995). At its most simple, this is a set of neurons in circuits, "engineered" (phylogenetically and ontogenetically) into three layers. The first layer accesses new data from the senses. This then checks for *recognition* against the middle, second layer of the sandwich: "*Ah, that's a face: friendly, unfriendly, potential mate, potential predator, etc.*". Level 2 moves "down" to compare its probabilistic predictions for "surprise" against level 1 input (faces are round and have edges), and "up" against level 3 models of the world (a round object that speaks, has eyes, nose, etc. is almost certainly a face).

Level 3, the *generative* or thinking and dreaming layer, likewise performs inference on level 2. It generates hypotheses, and makes predictions based on prior expectations. These ideas from level 3 imprint and modify level 2 and are tested empirically when level 2 checks its *recognition* again with level 1. Where there is a lot of surprise, data will be sampled more closely and frequently. For a given level 1 and 2 input, we are constantly updating our surprise metric, based on predictions/expectations in level 3. All this happens so seamlessly it can seem as if we are predicting the future. For example, when, as above, catching a ball we are continuously predicting where the ball will be a few seconds on from now. Given the relative slowness of neuronal transmission, in cricket or baseball the striker has to predict the ball's trajectory before it leaves the bowler's or pitcher's hand. These processes assume longer and longer time frames as we ascend the neuronal hierarchy towards consciousness. Catching a ball happens seemingly instantly and reflexively. Thinking about ball-catching integrates experience over an accumulation of memories and observations.

As the Chinese proverb has it, the wise man knows what to ignore. The Helmholtz machine allows selective attention to specific data (and suppression of irrelevant "noise") to facilitate building efficient, accurate internal mental representations of the world which can be modified in the light of experience/evidence. That which is already familiar requires little or no attention, since it has already iteratively been rendered into an "internal world", which is a species-, social-, and person-specific model of the prevailing environment.

PREDICTION ERROR MINIMISATION

The Free Energy Principle holds that the brain's aim, like that of the organism as a whole, is to a) sustain homeostasis and b) resist the forces of entropy, and that these are achieved by procedures that minimise surprise. The brain's measure of surprise is "free energy", the discrepancy between sensory input and the top-down models generated to account for it. The brain works to reduce this "prediction error" and to bind energy into a number of stable states.

The negentropic brain minimises prediction error in two main ways:

a) *Action*, which gathers the relevant information to account for, and minimise, input/model discrepancy. Speech is action. Thus: "Did you hear that noise, or were my ears deceiving me?" (this interpersonal aspect of PEM will be developed in Chapter 3).

b) Generating more consonant "*posteriors*", i.e., continuous modification and revising priors on the basis of experience.

Here we must introduce two more relevant concepts: *parsimony* and *attractors*. Hopkins (2016) suggests there is an inherent trade-off between the precision of our sensory inputs and the complexity of the models we use to account for them. Parsimony in this context refers to the need to reduce the chaotic multiplicity of possible predictions to a number of stable "attractors". An attractor is the set of numerical values towards which a system tends to evolve, from a wide variety of starting conditions. Attractors in biology have "value", that is, are of relevance to the organism, and help with its project of survival, maintaining homeostasis, staying safe, enhancing foraging potential, reproduction, etc. In humans they reflect the affective life of the individual – what we want, hope for, fear, seek, desire, makes us feel good/bad, etc. These affective "preferences" can in an FEP framework be seen as expectations: to the extent that the actions we take fulfil them, they reduce free energy and surprise and are thus rewarding.

This brings the rather abstract and "cognitive" seeming FEP closer to the feelings, fears, desires, and relationships that are the lifeblood of psychotherapy. As we shall see later, they also point to possible pathology. Simple, yet accurate and modifiable, rubrics of our relationships and emotional life characterise health. Simp*listic* models which override, deny, or repress lived experience are dysfunctional; conversely, suffering can result from the inability to prune complexity, compromising the ability to discern what is in our best interests, or what we really want.

AN ATTACHMENT GLOSS

For the purpose of the later clinical discussion (Chapters 4 to 8), I will now add a brief attachment digression. Let's imagine our visual receptors detect a long thin object while out walking. Depending on context, or *likelihood* (Smith, Lane, Parr, & Friston, 2019), exteroceptive (tropical field or urban park?) and interoceptive (how anxious do our heart rate, sweat glands, etc. suggest we are feeling?), this object might, from a top-down point of view, be a potentially poisonous snake, or a harmless stick.

Prediction error minimising (PEM) will steer active inference – "Shall I look a little closer to make sure, or assume the worst and run away?" This describes a "secure attachment" response – a balanced attempt to match input with possible generative models of the world. In a UK park the stick is most unlikely to be a snake. In an Indian paddy field, it could well be.

A less secure response would be *hyper*activation, aka anxious attachment – "Treat all sticks as snakes" – or *hypo*activation, aka avoidant attachment – "Forget snakes, stick to sticks" – (cf. Mikulincer & Shaver, 2007). Each strategy may be understandable in the individual's developmental context, but maladaptive in the present moment, the former leading towards anxiety/depression, the latter to potentially fatal risk-taking. The Bayesian brain makes weighted predictions, based on attachment dispositions established in childhood. Together with these later experiences – adverse or benign – these determine the "settings" of these predictions. The more secure the individual, the more able he or she will be to revise these in the light of experience.

The flux of time is integral to the Bayesian schema. The future arrives in the present – and becomes the past. Time moves at different rates in the brain's hierarchy: fast in a "reflex" low level of PEM, which may be life-saving (leap back and the snake misses its strike); slowly at higher cognitive levels where judgements are made ("Why am I so jumpy?", or "Better be careful next time I come this way and wear safer footwear"). In this way, probabilistic predictions are revised into more adaptive posteriors.

A further useful, if oversimplified, distinction

is between the worlds of people whose predictive dispositions classify them as *orchids* or *dandelions* (Boyce, 2019). The former (about 20 per cent in community samples) are hyper-responsive: in favourable environments they flourish, in unfavourable ones they fear they may wither and die. "Dandelions" are relatively insensitive to environmental influence, doing less well than "orchids" in good ones, but are somewhat impervious to unfavourable influences. Faced with stick/snake dilemmas it is in orchids' Bayesian interest to assume the worst, that snake-bite equals death. Dandelions can risk being more cavalier – there are effective antidotes to most snake-bites.

The relevance of these predictive strategies to psychotherapy is that orchids are more likely than dandelions to find themselves in need of psychological help (that is, are over-represented in clinical settings), but are also more likely to do well when that help is available (cf. Belsky, Bakermans-Kranenburg, & van Ijzendoorn, 2007). The general point is that our Bayesian predictive apparatus – which can be thought of as the self in action – is multiply determined by genetic endowment, the residues of developmental processes, and prior experience. The more conscious we are of this self – and the less *un*conscious – the more adaptive our predictions are likely to be.

CONCLUSION

Although FEP is mathematical, psychological, and informational, and says nothing specific about the architecture of the brain, it has strong neuroanatomical and neurochemical support (Badcock, Friston, Maxwell, & Ramstead, 2019; Parr & Friston, 2018). The histology of the cortex reveals six distinct layers that plausibly process data before handing them on in a modified form to adjacent layers. There is especially good evidence that this applies to the visual system. There are more downward neurones supplying the retina than those transmitting impulses upwards towards the visual cortex (Carhart-Harris & Friston, 2010).

At each level, conditional expectations (top-down priors) are encoded in deep pyramidal cells which suppress errors at the level below, while superficial pyramidal cells (bottom-up) convey errors forwards to revise expectations at the level above (Gu, Hof, Friston, & Fan, 2013).

The model is also consistent with the Hebbian principle of "fire together, wire together". As Friston puts it (2010, p. 132): "When the presynaptic predictions and postsynaptic prediction[s] are highly correlated, the connection strength increases." This suggests a role for the quotidian and developmental synaptic "pruning" seen in sleep and neurodevelopment, by which cerebral unruliness is reduced and parsimony reinforced (Hobson & Friston, 2012; Hobson, Hong, & Friston, 2014; Hopkins, 2016). Chapter 5 will suggest that psychoanalytic dream analysis facilitates these processes.

FEP does not just operate unconsciously. FEP conceives consciousness as an emergent phenomenon, arising as brain-life ascends the nested active inference hierarchy (Friston, Fortier & Friedman, 2018) and the role of complex self-representations begins to crystallise out (Graziano, 2019). We can extrapolate from what happens at the sensory level to higher functions and abstract thinking, and how the mind consciously reflects on its own processes. At every level, the simplest, most informationally efficient mental/neural representations are the best, and will prevail by natural selection.

The FEP can be thought of as "conversational" in the sense that top-down priors or generative models *converse* with the bottom-up sensations from the outside world (exteroception) or the body (interoception). Their interactions then reach consensus or agreement by minimising the discrepancies or "errors" which their encounter throws up. This process goes on continuously and seamlessly at multiple levels in the ascending and descending neuronal pathways of the brain.

Finally, we cannot depart this attempted exposition of PEM without mentioning the so-called "dark-room problem" (Clark, 2016; Friston,

Thornton & Clark, 2012). If the brain's main aim is to minimise surprise and bind energy at all costs, what's to stop us retreating into entirely predictable, sensation-minimised environments? But adaptation to complex environments requires us to make *choices*. We have to trade off easily available food against the foraging for stuff of higher nutritional value, choose suitable mates from a range of options, and generally need to cope with ever-changing environments. Affordances rest in the mid-zone between familiarity and novelty. "Goldilocks" attention is found in babies who attend least to total predictability or absolute chaos, but are turned on by manageable degrees of novelty (Kidd, Piantadosi, & Aslin, 2012). The presence of a trusted other enhances this novelty-seeking and exploration.

A related issue is how the seemingly conservative schema of FEP conceives the place of excitement, exploration, innovation, and creativity. Where do Panksepp's basic emotions of *play* and *seeking* fit in (Panksepp & Solms, 2012) with the

FEP model of the mind? Given that risk-taking and novelty-seeking are at their height in adolescence and early adulthood, one answer is that the brain needs to build up a repertoire of *survival scenarios* in order to match the likely risks with which its owner will be confronted in the course of a lifetime. Prediction error minimisation is continuously finessed against novelty so that we can go through the prior–posterior revision that improves adaptation. Since energy-binding is "rewarding" – via the dopaminergic system – PEM is powerfully motivating. When we are demotivated, or energy-minimising procedures are compromised by defective agency, chronic negative affective states presage psychological illness. Psychotherapy attempts to create the "duet for one" conditions where surprise becomes allowable and ultimately pleasurable – not least, as we shall see, in the form of healing tears.

Psychoanalytic resonances

Let's turn to an everyday example of the Bayesian brain in action, hoping, with its help, to link PEM with some familiar psychoanalytic themes.

One fine spring morning, in the course of a daily run across agricultural land, I noticed that the farmer had recently sprayed weedkiller. There was an unpleasant sickly smell, eliciting slight nausea, bringing to mind a mild feeling of illness I'd had at a similar time the previous year. The next day, following the same course, the smell had gone, but I noted in my *peripheral vision* a dark flapping object. My first thought was that this was a bird, perhaps a crow, affected by yesterday's poison. I turned my head to engage *central vision*, then *approached* to investigate further and if necessary rescue the corvid. The closer I came, however, the putative stricken bird revealed itself to be no more than a fragment of wind-blown black plastic, part of a discarded fertiliser bag.

This trivial incident illustrates a number of FEP and Bayesian principles.

- The stimulus was *ambiguous*, and therefore subject to high levels of *error* and potentially "free energy".

- The "*prior*", or meaning, attributed to this experience was based on *selective sampling* in peripheral vision together with recalled interoceptive nausea, leading to a top-down construct of "sick bird". This memory-based construction of an ambiguous stimulus could be deemed as an example of *transference*.

- In order to resolve the ambiguity, free energy minimisation (FEM) was required, via a) *action* – turning my head and moving

towards the flapping object in order to reduce "noise", and increase the *precision* of sensory sampling, and
b) *hypothesis revision* – "The poison will have dispelled by today so it would be odd if the bird were still affected".

- *Active inference* led to a stable "*posterior*": a free energy-minimised representation of reality, external ("It's only flapping plastic") and internal ("No nausea; no illness").
- *Parsimony* had generated two possibilities: sick bird, or plastic bag; the latter prevailed. Flap (surprise) became no-flap. Free energy was once more bound.

All of this went on semi-consciously. For most of the time prediction error/surprise-minimisation happens below awareness. It was my concurrent puzzling over the FEP and its relevance to psychotherapy that brought all this to conscious awareness, and to conversing first with myself, and now you, the reader, about it.

BION AND FEP

Let's go back from odd bird occurrences to the crying child. At times the caregiver is there on demand; at others inexplicably delayed. In order to make good predictions, a *theory of mind* is needed. The Bayesian brain gradually, and with help, learns to infer the causes, affects, motivations, and meanings which shape the child's interpersonal world – that is, to mentalise. Prediction error is built into this calculus; this will steer *actions*, aiming to minimise mistakes and, via *belief updating*, increase the chances of those predictions corresponding to the affordances of the world in which the child finds herself:

> "Mummy, I had a tummy ache last night. I called you, but you didn't come! I thought you had gone away."

> "Oh, sorry, darling, that sounds horrid and scary! I must have been fast asleep. If

*it happens again just come through and
wake me up." (cf. Allen, Bendixsen, Fenerci,
& Green, 2018)*

Here, the child is being taught the role of action ("*come through*"), affect co-regulation ("*Sorry
– how horrid*"), and how to generate relevant hypotheses or priors ("*Maybe she's asleep and can't hear
me*"). Note the *conversational* or narrative aspect of
prior–posterior interplay. Vis-à-vis the physical
world, action is used to clarify the discrepancy between the brain's model of the world and what the
environment is telling it – not a bird, just black plastic. In the interpersonal world, this dialogue is not
so much with physical objects – moving one's head
to get a better view, etc. – but with other people,
engaged in a joint project of reciprocal speech acts.

This takes us in the direction of developmental
and interpersonal themes with which psychoanalysis can begin to engage. We have already seen
how FEP parallels Freud's early speculations about
neural "energy". Common ground too is the reso-

nance with Bion's (1962) picture of how maternal reverie and alpha function (i.e., reservoir of priors) help the baby "process" raw experience. In the example, the mother put words to her child's fear ("*How scary darling*"). In FEP terms she is providing top-down input which helps bind free energy and resolve prediction error (cf. Mellor, 2018).

This *borrowed brain* (Holmes & Slade, 2017) model – the baby "borrows" the mother's brain to make sense of her experience – introduces an interpersonal dimension to the Bayesian process. Parents who are good at mentalising tend to have secure infants (Meins, Fernyhough, Fradley, & Tuckey, 2001). They readily put themselves in the child's shoes, and can see that what from an adult perspective might seem trivial – a mother momentarily inaccessible – to a small child would feel dangerous and trigger abandonment anxiety. Parental mentalising – understanding and resonating with their infants' affects – is initially non-verbal and implicit, communicated by facial expression, tone of voice, affiliative touch, swinging rhythms of soothing or stimulation. These embodied gestures present a model of the infant and her world from the caregiver's perspective. This helps the child to integrate primary sensory signals into regularities of emotional and interpersonal meanings (Fotopoulou & Tsakiris, 2017).

In this context of increasing predictability, the infant explores the environment, beginning with the mother's breast, and the minds of others, and with unconscious phantasies and proto-representations starts to build her own repertoire of Bayesian priors (e.g., "good breast", "bad breast" (cf. Hopkins, 2016)). With the help of predictable input from the caregiver, the infant brain begins to differentiate self- versus non-self generated sensations, initiating a sense of agency and early selfhood. Where that help is less predictable, absent, or perverse, psychopathology looms.

Bion's ideas map onto FEP in three main ways. First, "phantasy" can be thought of as a reservoir of top-down priors, while reality is encoded in bottom-up messages from the body, internal and external. An overlap with psychoanalysis lies in the concept of boundaries, implicit in the negentropy model. Living entities possess a statistically permeable boundary across which occur "conversational" exchanges – material and informational – with the environment. This boundary demarcates any system or creature from the milieu in which it is immersed. Inside this boundary, the "inner world" contains or implies a model of the environment and the organism's place within it – a "self"; however primitive or unconscious that representation might be.

In the theatre of the mind, and with the help of prostheses such as telescopes, microscopes, and other artificial inference machines, we extend consciousness to the outer reaches of the universe and down to the smallest imaginable particles. But ultimately the world can only be known via its impact on the sensory epithelium, and the beliefs entailed by active inference that such sensations evoke. Following Freud, Bion proposed a "contact barrier" between conscious

THE BRAIN HAS A MIND OF ITS OWN

and unconscious thought, ensuring that phantasy is sharply differentiated from reality, and the pleasure from the reality principles. Markov blankets apply throughout the nervous system's hierarchy from the sensory epithelia up to the level of conscious/unconscious interface. The blanket is the Bayesian equivalent of Bion's contact barrier (Kirchhoff, 2017; Kirchhoff, Parr, Palacios, Friston, & Kiverstein, 2018).

A third link with Bion concerns the interpersonal nature of experience, and his concept of communicative projective identification in which the mother feels on behalf of her child. In a prescient footnote (1911b, p. 302) Freud states:

> *It will rightly be objected that an organism which was a slave to the pleasure principle and neglected the reality of the external world could not maintain itself alive for the shortest time ... this is however justified when one considers that the infant* – provided one includes with it the care it receives

from its mother – *does almost realise a psychical system of this kind. (my emphasis)*

Seen through a Markov blanket darkly, the "world" of the isolated individual can only be inferred, never directly experienced. But in the interpersonal universe, initially of caregiver and infant, we encounter reality face to face, and can begin to know ourselves as we are known. Believing determines seeing, and for beliefs to be meaningful they are interpersonal, transmitted via the caregiver and the wider culture. Where "epistemic trust" (Fonagy & Allison, 2014) between child and caregiver is in question, this Bionic borrowed brain model breaks down. Deprived of the mother's triangulation, such children are on their own, and at the mercy of maladaptive beliefs. All this will be expanded in the next chapter.

Relational neuroscience

Thus far the discussion has centred on an isolated Bayesian brain trying to comprehend, operate, and survive in an entropic universe – somewhat remote from the concerns of the average psychotherapist! Moving closer to the real world, this chapter examines what happens when two such Bayesian brains collaborate.

A strong strand in contemporary neuroscience conceives the self as embodied, enactive, and *hy-*

per-social (Kyselo, 2014; Seth, 2013). Friston and Frith (2015) describe the maths of two-person PEM, using joint birdsong as a paradigm. They base their discussion on the phenomenon of "sensory attenuation" (Brown, Adams, Parees, Edwards, & Friston, 2013), in which sensory feed-forward is inhibited during action in order to preclude the logjam which would arise if bottom-up were to meet top-down *in media res*.

Sensory attenuation underpins "turn taking", a fundamental feature of human interactions, whether verbal or non-verbal (Holler, Kendrick, Casillas, & Levinson, 2015). On the whole one can either listen or talk, but not both. But if two inter-acting agents, drawing on the mirror neuron system, mutually assume the other is "like" themselves, *the energetic boundaries between them are temporarily dismantled*. Together they build a "shared brain" or "niche" (Constant, Ramstead, Veissiere, Camp-bell, & Friston, 2018), capable of active inference and prior–posterior revision. As John listens, Gill's speech can be subjected to PEM as though it arose

in John himself, and a similar process applies to
Gill vis-à-vis John. As they learn from one another,
their brain architecture and memory systems are
mutually modified. The resulting synchrony is
reminiscent of the psychoanalytic notion of the
"third" (Ogden, 1994), an idea, a feeling, an image,
arising between two intimate participants (i.e., analyst and analysand), contributed to by both, but
pertaining to neither. As Friston and Frith put it,
this produces a *duet for one*, or

> *… collective narrative that is shared among
> communicating agents (including one-
> self). For example, when in conversation
> or singing a duet, our beliefs about the
> (proprioceptive and auditory) sensations
> [bottom-up] we experience are based upon
> expectations about the song [top-down].
> These beliefs transcend agency in the sense
> that the song (e.g., hymn) does not belong
> to you or me. (2015, p. 14)*

Clinically, this insight is regularly exploited by therapists when using role play in couple and family therapy, or in individual work to explore the varying voices which inhabit our inner worlds. By interchanging roles, participants learn *both* to listen and to act, and are thus liberated from being trapped in fixed positions of, for example, the understanding one, the feeling, suffering, or inflicting one, etc.

The FEP/PEM point here is that the presence of a trusted other whose brain is temporarily on loan releases the sufferer from chronic prediction error. Where development proceeds smoothly this will be the parent, friend, lover, or partner. Where not, a psychotherapist fulfils this role. The next section expands on the neurobiology of borrowed-brain relationships.

BIOBEHAVIOURAL SYNCHRONY

Barrett (2017) argues that the FEP represents a profound challenge to Western culture's endemic

therapist
↑ child

"essentialism". The psychoanalytic expression of this is the famous Winnicott aphorism (1960), presaged by the Freud (1911b) footnote (above, page 54) that "there's no such thing as an infant, only an infant and mother together". As Barrett sees it, individuals, their brains, and their emotions are not static entities, but nodes in an ever-shifting chain of interconnected processes. In her analysis of pre- and perinatal mother–infant dyads, Feldman (2015b) describes these processes of *biobehavioural synchrony* as:

> ... *a co-wiring of parents' and infants' brains and behaviour into a synchronous unit that supports the infants' brain growth and buttresses social competencies. (p. 387)*

This entrainment of baby and mother brains – the correlations, correspondence, and mutual regulation of physiology, behaviour, and affect – begins in utero (Feldman, 2015a). Post-partum, synchrony applies at many levels: neural (via mirror neurons), physiological (heart rates), and hormonal (oxytocin). At a behavioural level, synchrony is evident in mirroring and playful/amorous interactions. The starting point for these complex mother–infant feedback loops begins with the release of maternal oxytocin in late-stage pregnancy and parturition. Oxytocin plays a key role in establishing and maintaining affectional bonds, priming the mother to interact with her baby via eye-to-eye mutual gaze, ready and accurate responsiveness to cues, adjusting her voice and touch to the baby's needs, and through close, soothing, and affectionate physical contact. Schore (2019) links these with vision-mediated right-brain-to-right-brain responsiveness of infant and mother. These hormonal and neuronal processes in the infant mean that the child feels increasingly connected to and familiar with the parent.

Moment to moment behavioural entrainment, parent–infant proximity and touch set off a cascade of reactions in parental and child brains.

Oxytocin is released as pulses, with maternal surges inducing oxytocin in the infant and vice versa:

> *Oxytocin functionality is transferred from parent to child via repeated experiences of social synchrony. (Feldman, 2015b, p. 388)*

[Oxytocin "cross-talks" to other hormonal and neurochemical systems, especially the fear system (amygdala), and dopaminergic reward system. Feldman sees this sub-cortical triangle of *protective bonding* (oxytocin), *pleasure/reward* (dopaminergic), and *fear* (amygdala) as the neuroanatomical and endocrine basis of the psychoanalytic unconscious. The prefrontal cortex (PFC) is connected to all three networks and provides modulatory regulation that balances them. With the help of the PFC, top-down priors minimise limbic and related bottom-up prediction errors, activated by incoming sensory input.]

Biobehavioural synchrony is not confined to mother–infant relationships, but has also been demonstrated in both primary and secondary caregiving fathers (Feldman, 2015b) as well as non-biological parents. While typically fathers serve different and later roles in infants' development, the male brain is sufficiently plastic to adjust to the demands of direct infant care if necessary, and, like its female counterpart, will secrete oxytocin.

Our species' physiological systems have evolved multiple pathways and buffering systems to ensure survival in a variety of differing circumstances and conditions. Nevertheless, biobehavioural synchronies are clearly vulnerable to dysfunction. Caspi, Moffitt and co-workers' (Caspi et al., 2002) thirty-year follow-up study showed that cumulative stressful life events in childhood (*adverse childhood experiences*, ACEs) are associated with enhanced risk of depression in adulthood. But not all children are similarly affected; it seems likely that those with "long" serotonin transporter genes (5-HTTLPR) are more resistant to adversity than those with the short variant. Primate (Suomi, 2016) and human studies show that these short-allele, "orchid" individuals, when in *favourable environments*, flourish *more* than their "dandelion" counterparts with long alleles.

For psychotherapists this means that the very vulnerabilities that bring people for help may also increase their responsiveness to the benign influences of therapy. Although clients seeking psychotherapeutic help are often those damaged by early adversity, neuroplasticity in this *ecological susceptibility model* (Belsky & Pluess, 2009) inspires therapists to feel confident that, given the right circumstances – including not just the therapy itself but the client's environmental context – flourishing is still possible.

Let's return to "duets for one", and the shared PEM they enable. Familiar dyads (parent–child, siblings, romantic partners, friends) synchronise with and mirror each others' biology and behaviour (Saxbe & Repetti, 2010). Secure attachment transmits "epistemic trust" as a springboard for social and physical exploration across the life cycle. Coan (2016) and colleagues (Coan, Schaefer, & Davidson, 2006) studied happily married couples using a "hand-holding" paradigm. The wives were exposed to stress – the threat of a mild electric shock — while in an fMRI scanner. Markers of HPA axis arousal (a measure of stress) were minimal or non-existent when holding their husbands' hands as compared with facing the threat on their own. Coan (2016) confesses to being puzzled by this "dog that didn't bark in the night" result: he'd expected a more active brain response to the husband's presence. But from an FEP perspective, PEM is facilitated in these dyadic scenarios. On one's own, it is adaptive to go for a fast-track (Kahneman 2011), "danger" mode in which top-down priors override low-precision sensory input: "Let's assume a stick's a snake". In the duet-for-one scenario, the potential unbound energy of threat is minimised by sharing the experience with a borrowed-brain pain-free companion. Sensory sampling can be more thoughtfully matched with possible top-down responses – such as trusting that "the experimenter is not really going to do anything really nasty to us".

Biobehavioural synchrony research shows that the greater the synchrony in the first year of life, the more pro-social, exploratory, and less anxious the child is likely to be at school entry (Feldman, 2015a, 2015b). Psychotherapy clients have typically had reduced periods of collaborative learning in their developmental histories, or, worse, attachment bonds reinforced not by collaboration and pleasure but by aversive stimuli (Hofer, 2002). The latter can be thought of as the negative aspect of brain borrowing in that a child may internalise a negative self-narrative, based on maternal depression, splitting, and resentment (Ginot, 2015).

There is as yet no specific experimental evidence on therapist/patient biobehavioural synchrony. But "common factors" of most therapies include a warm, calm, quiet, interruption-free, consistent, predictable, regular, reassuring therapeutic ambiance. These reproduce and evoke some of the biobehavioural aspects of secure mother–infant relationships. Therapists provide, metaphorically, the sensitive touch, or "caress" (Barratt, 2019) so lacking in their clients' developmental experience.⟩

People suffering with personality disorders are typically on a hair trigger for overwhelming anxiety (Allen, Fonagy, & Bateman, 2008). For them fast, rather than slow thinking is the norm (Kahneman, 2011). They are in the grip of perceptual distortion and ingrained prediction errors, driven by the need to bind free energy into a modicum of predictability, however dysfunctional. An early psychotherapeutic task is to re-establish a degree of biobehavioural synchrony. The patterns and rhythms of therapy help with this, as do the joint attention and affective mirroring typical of secure attachments. But the more disturbed the individual, the more problematic this is likely to be; such trust remains a fragile and fluctuating flower which varies from session to session and moment to moment within sessions. Identifying, understanding, and overcoming obstacles to biobehavioural synchrony are preconditions for effective psychotherapeutic work.

CRITICAL PERIODS

A related theme in social neuroscience is that of critical or *sensitive periods* (Feldman, 2015a; Tottenham, 2014). These are windows in the developmental processes where environmental influence and therefore neuroplasticity are at their most salient. Neurohormonal components in sensitive periods include the prefrontal cortex (PFC) the amygdala, and the HPA axis and cortisol system. The mother's presence influences both the development of the amygdala and the infant's exploratory behaviours (Cunningham & Brosch, 2012). Securely attached infants in the presence of their mothers are less frightened by a "visual cliff", and have lower salivary cortisol levels, compared with insecure or mother-absent counterparts. During sensitive periods, the presence of mother strengthens and tones the PFC–amygdala link. If the mother is stressed, or in parent-deprived children (e.g., Romanian orphans), the buffering and cortisol-level lowering impact of parental presence is reduced. Their neuroplasticity diminished, these children are more anxious, less adventurous, and more prone to anxiety disorders (Rutter, 2012).

Animal models support these observations. Rat pups in the presence of their mothers find new odours interesting and attractive, while mature rats become odour aversive. Mother-deprived rats are odour aversive from the start, and as adults are generally less exploratory and more reactive to novelty (Tottenham, 2014). The presence of the mother in the sensitive period enables these infants, when mature, to be more mature and exploratory.

Children whose parenting has been interrupted or sub-optimal may appear more mature than those where continuous and consistent parenting has prolonged the sensitive period in which these relational buffering effects are active. Such children may have a preternatural sense of self. Their accelerated development is adaptive in that caution and threat-aversive strategies are needed in the absence of a buffering caregiver, but can have the long-term negative consequences of an over-

or underactive HPA axis and impaired emotion processing.

Therapy entails reopening a sensitive period in clients' lives so that the suffering patient is responsive to the affect-modulating presence of a caregiver. Under the aegis of entrainment and biobehavioural synchrony, the neuroplasticity needed for new relationship constellations becomes activated. The borrowed brain of the therapist begins to modulate unstable PFC/amygdala cortisol-mediated flight/fright tendencies. A playful inner and outer dialogue becomes possible, sometimes for the first time. This is Kris's (1952) "regression in the service of the ego", a feature of artistic creativity as well as psychotherapy: an opportunity for reworking the self, so that it becomes more encompassing, more coherent, and imbued with an authentic sense of agency. In mental health practice, this optimism must confront the disturbances and dysfunctions in PEM found in psychopathology, and it is to these we now turn.

4

Free energy and psychopathology

The Bayes model suggests that free energy minimisation evolved as an adaptation to inherently unpredictable environments, a bulwark against entropic processes, and a springboard for flourishing in the social milieu constitutive of our species. Implicit however is the inherent fragility of negentropy. In an entropic world, as the Red Queen famously puts it, "*It takes all the running you can do to stay in the same place. If you want to get somewhere you must run twice as fast ...*" (Carroll, 1871).

This fragility, arguably, is the basis of psychological illness/psychopathology. Things can go wrong in a number of different ways. First, there is the ever-present danger of trauma. Despite the best laid plans, unpredictable, unforeseen, and deleterious environmental impingements can overwhelm PEM. As Freud repeatedly put it:

> *We describe as "traumatic" any excitations from outside … powerful enough to break through the protective shield … and result in permanent disturbances of the manner in which the energy operates … (1925d, p. 3),* and

> *… these systems are not in a good position for binding the inflowing amounts of excitation and the consequences of the breach in the protective shield follow all the more easily. (1920g, p. 609)*

This is especially relevant in people suffering from the *adverse childhood events* mentioned earlier – neglect, devastating losses, emotional, physical, and/or sexual abuse. As Freud suggests, what makes trauma traumatic is the piercing of the defensive shield that protects the self, dividing the entropy of the external world from the living order within (Garland, 2002). Trauma is by definition unexpected, unpredictable, non-contingent, and often violent. Psychological trauma hurts because painful "negative valence" (Joffily & Coricelli, 2013) arises in situations of chronic un-minimised prediction error. Freud's definition of trauma points to an absence of top-down models with which to bind upcoming free energy.

⌐ In therapy, traumatic memories are reawakened in the therapeutic relationship. For someone who has suffered severe neglect or a devastating bereavement, a holiday break on the part on the therapist may be experienced as a sudden death, the gaps between sessions felt as out-of-mind neglect. But because the event is now *jointly enacted*, and available for *shared* PEM, it can be brought into the "area of omnipotence" (Winnicott, 1965; Casement, 1981). Mutually mentalised, the unbound energy associated with loss or violence becomes containable.⌐

A second vulnerability factor for psychopathology arises when the capacity for active inference is compromised. Minimising prediction errors depends on a dynamic interaction ("conversation") between top-down models and bottom-up signals in which the inherent error in both directions is taken into account. This depends on "precision weighting". As discussed in Chapter 1, active inference entails a) agency and b) prior–post generative model revision. Agency enhances the precision of sensory input – "Let's see if that's a sick bird or just flapping plastic". Model revision depends on balancing the accuracy of bottom-up sensations against available meanings – "I'm probably only thinking it's a sick bird because I felt ill yesterday".

Both agency and model revision skills are acquired and honed in the course of development, and therefore vulnerable to environmental disruption. Children adapt to the prevailing circumstances of their family ecology. FEP insists that surprise must be minimised at all costs. Given adverse developmental circumstances, the homeostatic imperative means reducing complexity in simplistic and anachronistic ways, inhibiting and restricting risk-taking and the "negative capability" needed to revise predictions in the light of experience.

In line with attempts to move psychiatric diagnosis from purely descriptive phenomenology to neuroscience-based constellations, FEP enthusiasts are beginning to formulate aspects of psychiatric illness in prediction error terms. Following the Helmholtz model described in Chapter 1, PEM can go wrong in one of two ways. First, valid sensory information can be overridden by simplistic and/or anachronistic top-down models. Conversely, there can be excessive precision attributed to sensory input, at the expense of the generative models of the world. Schematically, these "prediction error errors" map onto psychosis and autism respectively.

It has been suggested (Van Os, 2009) that psychoses, and especially schizophrenia, be thought of as "salience dysregulation syndromes". The term "salience" here can be seen in prediction error terms as over-weighting generative models, rendering them impervious to non-confirmatory bottom-up experience. Thus, despite evidence to the contrary, in paranoid delusions the world is felt to be freighted with malevolent significance.

Ermakova et al. (2018) have shown that psychosis sufferers do indeed have impaired prediction error processing. They compared psychosis patients with neurotypicals while being monitored in an fMRI scanner. The subjects were asked to choose between two images in order to get a monetary reward. In one condition the subject needed to modify their predictions to obtain the reward. In the other, the rewards were allocated randomly. In the condition where they had to modify their predictions in the light of experience, the psychosis sufferers did less well, but not in the random choice set-up. The psychosis sufferers' fMRIs showed significant differences in prediction from neurotypicals in error signalling between the midbrain and the right dorsolateral prefrontal cortex. Bottom-up (midbrain) communication/conversation with top-down cortical models was impaired, especially in the dopaminergic pathways, which are implicated in psychosis.

The argument is that neurochemical abnormalities in delusions impact the signal/noise "gain" in the PEM process, so that possible model imprecisions are discounted, for example:

"My house is beset by snakes."

"But have you actually seen one? Couldn't they just be sticks?" [What about the bottom-up evidence?]

"No, but I just know *they're lurking out there." [Irrespective of evidence, I'll hang onto what my top-downs tell me.]*

This points to possible mechanisms by which psychotic beliefs might persist despite evidence to the contrary. PEM underwrites the psychiatric maxim that it is counterproductive to try to argue people out of their delusions. Acceptance of the validity of clients' experience is a precondition for progress to a higher level of the PEM hierarchy where the possibility of illness *can* be jointly entertained, without clashing with lower-level faulty inferences.

If psychosis represents dysfunction in top-down prediction error minimisation, FEP sees autism as the converse. Here there is "enslavement to the senses" in which the inherent noisiness of sensory input is discounted. The capacity to contextualise and attend only to relevant input is offline, while mentalising – thinking about thinking – and hence subjecting sensory data to relevance criteria, is in abeyance.

Importantly, the FEP model applies as much to *interoception* as to exteroceptive input (Duquette & Ainley, 2019). The brain, top-down, has to account for the sensations it receives not just from the external world but also from in the body: heart, lungs, gut, genitals, limbs, etc. Ongaro & Kaptchuk (2018) see somatisation disorders in terms of inference procedures in which excessive precision weighting is attributed to interoceptive sensations. This is for two reasons: first, one's bodily sensations are taken as more "precise" than those gathered from an ever-changing environment; second, because they are typically organised as *"habits" rather than hypotheses* and thus – in the manner of a "stubborn scientist" (Yon, de Lange, & Press, 2019) – are inaccessible to top-down revision. Maladaptively reducing prediction error entails matching over-weighted interoceptive input – raised heart rate, breathlessness, fleeting pains – with rigid fearful or depressive priors. This sets up a vicious circle which further reinforces anxiety-producing interceptions.

As Ongaro & Kaptchuk (2018) put it:

> *All symptoms are products of an inferential process that is never strictly reducible to physiological dysfunction and is sometimes only loosely related or unrelated to it. "Explained" and "unexplained" symptoms thus lie on a continuum … (p. 3)*

Mood disorders can likewise be conceptualised within the interoceptive FEP framework (Barrett, 2017; Badcock, Davey, Whittle, Allen, & Friston, 2017). According to the *social risk hypothesis*, depression is typically triggered by loss, either actual or symbolic. In a "double whammy", loss triggers emotional pain; meanwhile the very person with whom that pain could, via the attachment dynamic, be co-regulated is no longer there. The brain/mind is flooded with potentially entropic sensations as the familiar secure base is stripped away. Loss of appetite, anxiety, sleep disturbance, and social withdrawal represent attempts at dampening down unminimised free energy. This PEM entails clinging to a depressive world view, rather than risking disconfirmatory actions (including hope-engendering conversations with therapists) and modifications of depressive priors. There is free-energy minimised safety in pain, compared with exploration: "Children always keep a-hold of nurse, for fear of meeting something worse" (Belloc, 1907).

Rescued suicides describe how despair gives

way to preternatural calm resolve before embarking on suicidal acts. Hamlet asks himself (mixed-metaphorically) whether "to suffer the slings and arrows of outrageous fortune/ Or take up arms against a sea of troubles, and by opposing, end them". "Outrageous fortune" equates to energy unbound. Hamlet's self-slaughter is at least *action* – in death he imagines himself safely aligned with the world's entropy, no better and no worse than nothingness. But then, "what dreams may come .../ must give us pause" – perhaps there is even greater chaos in store, beyond the everyday entropy of the known world. Secular therapeutic approaches offer less threatening top-down narratives: "This too will pass"; "With help, perhaps I'll feel different tomorrow".

OCD can be thought of in FE terms as fruitless striving for spurious certainties. In a riposte to Socrates's much-quoted aphorism that "The unexamined life is not worth living", Dennett reminds us that "The over-examined life is nothing much to write home about either" (2017, p. 278).

Thus far we have divided the free energy minimisation process into a broad-brush bottom-up/ top-down dichotomy. But the Friston model shows, neuroanatomically and mathematically, how reducing prediction error is a complex multi-level process. Bottom-up does not refer simply to activity at the sensory epithelia, but at each level of synaptic connection. Relevant here is the neurocomputational model of Emotional Awareness (EA) described by Smith and colleagues (2019a, 2019b). This differentiates three levels of emotion processing: a) automatic modulation of interceptive stimuli, b) representing emotions as felt affects, and c) a level of conscious emotional awareness, akin to mentalising, that enable appraisal, and choosing whether to be motivated by anger or fear, or to discount or tone down feelings. PEM is pertinent at each of these three levels, and Smith and co-workers point to the associations between psychopathology and impaired EA and the ways in which therapeutic interventions restore or enhance EA.

The Ermakova et al. study (2018) looked at PEM in midbrain–cortex interactions in psychosis.

Similarly, Lanius, Frewen, Tursich, Jetly, and McKinnon (2015) discuss MPFC/amygdala dissociation in post-traumatic states, arguing that in the absence of top-down input from the PFC, patients dampen amygdala activity by substance abuse or self-harm. Seeing negative affect in terms of un-minimised prediction errors (Joffily & Coricielli, 2013) helps us understand the salutary benefits of mindfulness. The meditator observes feelings of shame, fear, self-disgust, etc. as they arise and is encouraged to view these negative emotions as evanescent and to "let them go", like passing clouds, while retaining a degree of equanimity (Weng, Lapate, Stodola, Rogers, & Davidson, 2018). Thus are the weightings assigned to interoceptive sensations down-regulated, allowing PEM to proceed more smoothly.

SUMMARY

To summarise the discussion so far, psychopathology is conceived in the FEP framework as difficulties with active inference, due to a) impaired agency/

action and/or b) failure of model revision in the light of experience. These result from:

1. Over-weighting top-down inference (psychosis)
2. Over-weighting interoceptions (somatisation disorders, depression) or exteroceptions (autism)
3. Paucity of priors (trauma)
4. Repression of interoceptions, making them unavailable for conscious-level PEM (depression)
5. Difficulties with recruiting others in duets for one, and hence go-it-alone maladaptive PEM procedures (substance abuse, suicidal acts, personality disorders)
6. Inappropriate complexity procedures: oversimplistic priors (personality disorders), or failure to reduce complexity and hence inhibition of action (OCD).

Let's now consider how psychotherapy might work to remediate some or all of these.

Uncoupling top-down/bottom-up automaticity

If mental illnesses are diseases of social brains, then it is likely that evolution will have produced both natural and culturally mediated repair systems to reverse or mitigate them. In order to stave off entropy, living systems have evolved defences which help resist chaos, maintain structure, and enhance adaptation and survival (Connolly, 2018). In humans defences operate "all the way up", from the cellular level of the immune system, through the interpersonal attachment dynamic, to societal structures, ranging from social care to tidal barriers and military hardware. These, like the systems they are designed to protect, are initially involuntary and automatic but, prosthetically enhanced, become goal-directed societal formations. We share our immune system with fellow mammals, but the epidemiology of high-density communities, urbanisation, and migration mean that we need vaccination and immunisation programmes to augment our capacity to outwit disease.

This chapter examines some key themes of psychoanalytic therapies: free association, dream analysis, sexuality, transference, and mentalising. All depend on *uncoupling* the bottom-up and top-down components of PEM. This enables stimuli and sensations to be separated from the generative models they elicit. By prising apart the two directions of neuronal flux, and scrutinising their interactions, non-interactions, and inappropriate weightings, therapy opens up possibilities for more adaptive solutions. With sensation decoupled from inference, and in the presence of a modulating, moderating, affect-buffering therapist, surprise no longer spells danger but creatively adds to a sufferer's generative model repertoire. The greater the range of top-down predictions, the more the opportunities for binding energy and the less the need to resort to rigid, limited, or anachronistic strategies. Equally important is learning to listen to the "granularity" of incoming sensations, extrinsic and interoceptive. Introducing a therapeutic caesura in this way enhances the capacity of the patient to act on, adapt to, and shape his or her environment, including, via mentalising, the self itself.

DREAMS

Let's start from Freud's well-trodden yet still enigmatic "royal road". In sleep, and especially dream-sleep, bottom-up sensory input and top-down prediction are largely disarticulated. Exteroception is in abeyance, leaving the field clear for interoceptions – thirst, hunger, sexual arousal, pain, fear, etc. – and the plethora of top-down dream narratives which they call into being. The title of this essay derives from a phrase which came, ready made, into the author's mind immediately on waking, stimulated by a dream of delicious food, while facing the prospect of a low-calorie "5:2" (cf. Harrison, 2013) "starve" day. Whatever my mind's good intentions, the calorie-hungry brain insisted that what it wanted was a slap-up meal!

Dream interpretation forms an important focus of analytic work, albeit less perhaps than in its founder's day. Most dreams are forgotten within minutes of waking, and many people claim, erroneously (when REM-tracked in sleep laboratories), not to dream. Hobson and Friston (2012) suggest that during the hours of dark, prediction error inevitably increases, and with it the dangers of free energy, aka surprise. Evolution, they suggest, has serendipitously exploited this hazard in the circadian sleep–wake cycle. Even if we are no longer surrounded, like James's (1890) baby, by "blooming buzzing confusion", we nevertheless go through our days bombarded by sensory impressions, external and interoceptive. In the absence of afferent input, sleep allows potentially free-energetic – and so entropic – memory traces of the "day's residue" (Freud's term) to be consolidated into parsimonious (i.e., decomplexified) energy-bound representations. This rationalisation or neuronal pruning is a prime function of sleep.

Given the lack of exteroceptive input, Freud's formulation of dreams as wish fulfilments can be recast as the workings of desire (interoception-driven feelings) and their elaboration into top-down narratives. Although this view does not fully underwrite the Freudian notion of dreams as *disguised* wish fulfilments, it sees dream themes as value-laden, replete with affective significance. In the FEP model, dreaming has two main jobs. The first, as above, is "housekeeping", consolidating the worth-memorising wheat of the previous day's experiences from the discardable chaff (cf. Hopkins, 2016). The second, I suggest, is to generate a range of *pluripotential virtual reality scenarios*. Their purpose is to accumulate narratives able to encompass the vicissitudes and unpredictable varieties of experience, past and to come.

Dreams are typically populated by known "characters", but distinguished from waking experience by a degree of bizarreness, vagueness, and ambiguity, especially of faces. This lifts dreams from specificity and thereby increases their *valency*. The meaning and associations to a specific dream can always go in a number of different directions. The dream story and the language in which it is clothed is pluripotential, and thus applicable for PEM across a range of possible real-life happenings.

Here is an example:

> *John, a man in late middle age, dreamed that two sets of friends, both couples, living round the corner from one another, had jointly "downsized" and moved into a shared flat or apartment. While visiting them in their new abode, he surreptitiously picked up a chocolate Easter egg and ate it.*

Free associating to the dream brought a day's residue to mind. The previous evening, John had told an acquaintance that he and his wife were thinking of moving house to be nearer to their grandchildren.

> *"Oh dear, that's sad," had come the response – "but careful you don't drop off your perch; that's what often happens when people downsize."*

Freud's explanation for dreams' bizarreness was that desire, subject to the incest taboo and Oedipality, is necessarily disguised. He likened the bizarreness of dreams to packed ice, in which a number of salient themes are jammed one into the other. Disentangled, the dream's themes and linguistic tropes included:

- John's anxiety and mourning about the process of moving
- His fear of old age and eventual death, "just round the corner"
- The "flat"-ness and "downsizedness" of de-eroticised old age

- Compensatory self-soothing via oral gratification
- Egg metaphors: i) "curate's egg" of moving, its good and bad aspects, ii) "hatching" and hope of grandchildren.

From an FEP perspective, dreaming helps rework potentially traumatic free energy so that the associated terror can be "bound" and its concomitant mental pain made more tolerable and less disruptive. Top-down inferences, capable of linguistic representation, "bind" the energy associated with likely future fears – moving, changing, aging. By generating multivalent free-energy minimising priors they reduce prediction error. There is no escaping the emotional pain of loss, separation, and death, but if (to adapt Kipling) those "impostors" can be "met" with top-down priors, they will safeguard against, or at least postpone, entropic surprise.

AMBIGUITY AND TRANSFERENCE

In the "flapping black object" example in Chapter 2, an *ambiguous stimulus* presented itself to the subject, who saw something anomalous or "*untoward*" out of the corner of his eye. Given the imprecision of rod-based peripheral vision, this was interpreted in the light of a prior based on the previous day's experience – a possible poisoned bird. But following action – face-forward movement *towards* the object with foveal cones now activated – this was revised to a more everyday posterior, loose agricultural plastic. Recollecting this sequence in tranquillity, a somatising anxiety ("Could I have been poisoned by the weed spray?") shows how error-prone visual sensations, bound together with interoception-driven prior, produced a false perception ("It's got to be something, ah, yes, a sick bird"). A top-down picture of the world built from affectively salient past experience ("I felt ill, so maybe the bird does too") was carried over, or *transferred*, inappropriately, into an ambiguous present.

The ramifications of ambiguity are an important part of the FEP story in a number of ways. First, ambiguous stimuli capture our *attention*. If our prediction error minimising doesn't fully fit the facts, we keep coming back until we find a solution that does correspond. Deliberately ambiguous stimuli, as in well-known visual illusions such as the duck-rabbit picture or the Necker cube, are unresolvable because they evoke incompatible top-down-generated conclusions ("It's a duck", "No it's not, it's a rabbit", "Well it can't be both, so which is it? Better take yet another look"). Second, ambiguity is handled in a Bayesian fashion at different levels of the neuronal hierarchy. In the famous Müller-Lyer illusion, lines of identical length appear to differ depending on whether 45-degree "arrow-heads" at their ends diverge or converge. The illusion arises out of the normal "moon and sixpence" adjustments needed to take distance perception into account. The eye assumes the divergent lines imply distance, so the retina "tells" the visual cortex that it is a longer line, but situated farther away, and so only *seemingly* identical.

High-level knowledge is "probabilistically idle": knowing that the lines are in fact the same length does nothing to destroy the illusion when erroneous PEM occurs at lower levels of the hierarchy. Hohwy (2013) sees this as analogous to psychosis sufferers whose delusions and hallucinations are not affected by top-down acceptance that they are mentally ill. Only through therapeutic procedures that stimulate active inference, as in directly conversing with avatars held responsible for the delusions, does the hold of false beliefs begin to lessen (Craig et al., 2017).

An example of the hierarchical nature of PEM arose on a BBC radio programme on the topic of miracles. A priest was interviewed and claimed that "Miracles *do* happen. I was a drug addict, and now I'm a pastor." Miracles are by definition highly improbable events, which cannot be accommodated to ordinary top-down generative models. From a Bayesian perspective it is true that very few drug addicts become pastors. Finding an "explanation"

– minimising prediction error – entails moving either up, or down, the Markov blanket hierarchy. Upwards, extending the range of generative models, theology offers an explanatory framework – God works miracles. Downward towards enhanced "granularity" (see below), psychotherapy might suggest that "maybe under specific circumstances drug addicts *do* become pastors" – perhaps through encountering a sympathetic prison visitor, or finding a Gideon Bible beside one's hostel bed.

Psychoanalytic psychotherapy places the analysis of transference at the centre of its mutative method, seeing it as the persistence of childhood models of relationships into adult life and their re-enactment in the therapeutic relationship. As Loewald (1960) poetically puts it, when analysis is successful, persistent intrusive "ghosts" take their rightful place as "ancestors". Freud came to see that, as with illusions, mere intellectual challenge to transferential assumptions is usually ineffective: "[I]t is impossible to destroy anyone in absentia or in effigie" (1912b, p. 108). Transference is evoked, comes alive, and becomes available for scrutiny precisely because of the relative ambiguity which the therapist presents. For Laplanche (2009) the analyst is an "enigmatic signifier … the one who guards the enigma and provokes the transference".

Some aspects of therapists are self-evident – age, gender, tone of voice, ambience, qualifications, etc. But even these seemingly unambiguous details are coloured by top-down/transferential modelling. One patient, two years into analysis, suddenly noticed the analyst's wedding ring: "OMG, *have you just gone off and got married?*" In fact the ring had been there all along. The patient's emotional development was beginning to move from childlike exclusive dependence to a stage where his top-down models could contemplate, live with, and learn from Oedipal rivalry and exclusion.

Alongside these hidden-in-plain-sight revelations, the technical stance of reticence and anonymity, like the world glimpsed in peripheral vision, helps highlight the client's preconceptions, which then become available for scrutiny and reworking. As with the fuzziness of dream characters' faces, the analyst remains elusive and polyvalent, responding only with those aspects of herself which evoke salient meanings in the patient's life. As one novice therapist breathlessly announced during her coffee break, "I've finally realised that transference is real: my first patient today described me as a hideous witch; the second said I was a beautiful angel." Much analytic technique and training centres on the need to maintain and draw on that ambiguity for therapeutic ends (e.g., Patient: "*Have* you *got any children?*"; Analyst: "*That's a really interesting question – let's think about what might have prompted it to come up today?*").

This FEP explanation of transference can be compared with the art historian Gombrich's (1960) claim that ambiguity is central to the workings of art (cf. Kandel, 2012). Art objects re-present physical or emotional experience, yet are composed out of materials – pigment, brushstrokes, stone, metal, digital pulses, etc. – that bear no relationship to that which they depict. This illusory quality of art means that aesthetic experience is co-created between the artist and the mind/brain of an audience who project their feelings and past experience into the artefact.

A comparable case can be made for the psychotherapy session which has the quality of virtual reality in that it is both intensely experiential, dealing with the fundamentals of relational existence – love, loss, pain, sex, the body – and at the same time sequestered from real life, framed by the fifty-minute hour, the ambiguous presence of the therapist, and the non-consequential role of feelings engendered in the analytic space.

This brings us to another important aspect of FEP: its temporal aspect and how this relates to desire. Although seemingly instantaneous, our perceptions are time-bound. The sequence of sensations, stimulating priors, followed by error minimisation and posterior revision, can be translated into an affective train of tension, consummation, and resolution. In the example in Chapter 2, it was a relief to realise that the putative bird was but a figment of the imagination. The very binding of energy is rewarding. In Feldman's tripartite subcortical dynamic unconscious, based on attachment, reward, and anxiety, difficulties arise when the prefrontal cortex–midbrain PEM communication is disrupted. Anxiety without PFC modulation drives out reward, and stimulates the attachment dynamic that in turn inhibits exploration. Therapy deepens trust and discourages this premature and defensive closing down of surprise. Exploration of the ambiguity/certainty dialectic is satisfying and rewarding. After a "good" session, even if evoking much sadness and tears, both therapist and patient emerge feeling "better", with a sense of progress and hope.

Joffily and Coricelli (2013) show that experiencing negative emotions leads to reworking of memory, with enhancement of current experience, and down-weighting of stored priors. In a context of sadness, clients begin to allow themselves to acknowledge that their therapist does listen and care, despite top-down expectations to the contrary. Kashdan, Barrett, and McKnight (2015) describe how increasing this fine detail or "granularity" of experience enables one to sift positive from negative, and move on from defeat to learning from experience.

Put another way, ambiguity and its resolution is inherently *rewarding*. For Laplanche (1987) ambiguity and enigma are built into the developmental process. In his model the breast – its presence and absence – is a "sexual organ", but, for the naïve infant, one wrapped in mystery. The mother's loving sensuality in relation to her baby is suffused with a degree of eroticism which the baby cannot fully comprehend. Building on this idea, Target (2007; see also Fonagy, Gergely, Jurist, & Target, 2002) suggests that sexuality is the one exception to the finding that accurate affect-mirroring by caregivers underpins a child's sense of self. In the realm of genital exploration and proto-masturbation, parents typically distract, avoid, or punish rather than reflect the child's explorations and nascent sexuality. This leaves an enigmatic mirror-hunger, whose resolution is postponed until sexual life begins in adolescence and early adulthood. In the realm of sexuality there is an inherent reservoir of unbound or enigmatic energy, which can permeate the analytic consulting room in "erotic transference". With the top-down/bottom-up uncoupling that good psychotherapy technique ensures, this becomes available for joint mentalising, enabling clients to develop a clearer sense of the lineaments of their sexuality and desire.

MENTALISING

As part of the anti-entropic repair system, evolution, biological and cultural, has generated another level of the top-down/bottom-up hierarchy (Wilson, 2002). This is *meta-cognition*, the capacity to think about thinking, or to *mentalise* (Frith, 2012). Like brain function generally, mentalising can be thought of in Helmholtzian terms, as another level in the hierarchy of upward and downward streaming and prediction error minimising, in which the brain reflects on its own thought processes. Mentalising provides the opportunity to stand back from oneself and scrutinise one's active inference procedures, just as, at lower levels, prediction error is minimised by improved sensory sampling.

Frith (2012) argues that such meta-cognition is especially relevant to the cooperative or "we-mode" procedures, which occupy a great deal of human waking life. For cooperation to be effective we need to take account of the viewpoints and motivations of others, and likewise to factor in our own psychology and how it will be perceived by our fellow co-operators. Again, this is typically implicit and below consciousness. It is a remarkable fact of urban life that opposing pedestrians in busy streets rarely bump into one another: walkers make unconscious predictions about the direction of travel of others and self and all runs smoothly. Occasionally however this goes wrong: walker A goes left, aiming to avoid contact, just as walker B goes to his right with the same plan in mind. At this point, *explicit* mentalising, of both self and other and their interaction takes over, often with humorous acknowledgement, while each proceeds on his or her respective way.

Likewise PEM mostly goes on below conscious awareness. We take for granted the objects, processes, motivations, and meanings of our *Umwelt*, inanimate and animate. But occasional – or recurrent – incongruities, natural or contrived (e.g., optical illusions), as well as interpersonal impasse and conflict are unavoidable. These are typically resolved via "triangulation" – checking possibly false perceptions with a trusted other – "Did you hear a noise out there, or was I just dreaming?".

This triangulation is central to child development. Children develop "epistemic trust" (Fonagy & Allison, 2014) by repeatedly checking their perceptions and conceptions with caregivers. People suffering from borderline personality disorder (BPD) evince "epistemic hypervigilance". Lacking access to trusted others with whom to confirm or disconfirm their experiences, they are in a constant state of readiness to reject intimacy. A technique in the mentalising approach to psychotherapy with people suffering from BPD (Allen, Fonagy, & Bateman, 2008) is the procedure known as "pressing the pause button". Here, when problematic, therapist and client interrupt the flow of their interactions in order to examine "what was going on between us". This immediately disrupts automatic top-down/bottom-up pathways, making transferential thoughts and behaviours available for scrutiny.

Compare this with Berger's account of the artist at work:

> *To draw is to look, examining the structure of experiences. A drawing of a tree shows, not a tree, but a tree being looked at … A tree being looked at … not only takes minutes or hours … it also involves, derives from, and refers back to much previous experience of looking. (Berger, 1972, p. 17)*

The work of the consulting room has much in common with this. First, an "event" – for instance, a client's outburst of explicit or covert anger triggered by a therapist's holiday break, occupying no more than moments of clock time, may lead to extended collaborative reflection. Second, the discussion is likely to attend to "much previous" comparable interpersonal experience. The aim is to identify and modify both bottom-up and top-down procedures. Enhanced sensory sampling means that the client begins to tease out differences and the automatic assumptions these evoke, such as between a therapeutic break with a high probability of resumption, and a childhood history of being arbitrarily "dropped" by a divorcing parent. This scrutiny, if things go well, can lead to more realistic model revision about the non-irreversibility of losses.

FREE ASSOCIATION

The "enhanced sensory sampling" or granularity described above is a variant of what Barratt (2016) argues was Freud's greatest discovery, clinically and

theoretically: the concept and practice of "free association". Freud's (1916–17) image of this was that of
the passenger in a train looking out of a window and
observing the landscape as it flashes past. Barratt
questions the quasi-logical "en*train*ment" aspect of
this image. For him, free association captures the
spontaneous eruption of desire, untrammelled by
the representational influence of narrative coherence. In free association, thoughts, interoceptive
bodily sensations, impulses, and images enter the
mind "from below", available for observation and
later discussion. Setting top-down constructions
temporarily aside, the attentive, quiet, listening
therapist and patient collaboratively enter states
of free-floating attention and negative capability.
For Barratt (2019) the ebb and flow of this process
is in itself existentially liberating, quite apart from
the access to specific repressed, repudiated, or un-
awakened desires it provides.

Avoidant clients, with intellectual defences,
are both resistant to, and likely to benefit from
encouragement to free associate. With their

co-regulatory sensitive period reopened, they can explicitly think about repressed feelings and fears, which no longer have to be minimised for the sake of security. As in the Coan (2016) study, the potential for disruptive free energy associated with avoided feelings is mitigated by the therapist's calm presence. Conversely, those with anxious attachment strategies typically feel overwhelmed by the uprush of interoceptive bodily feelings. Here the job of free association is to slow things down so they can be identified and subjected to rational top-down scrutiny ("Could we consider the possibility that that horrible stomach pain you get whenever your husband goes on a trip doesn't necessarily spell gut cancer?").

THE SELF

Living organisms depend for their survival on a "sense of self". Even a unicellular creature such as an amoeba needs to "know where it is" vis-à-vis gradients of potential nutrients or adverse conditions.

In complex systems such as ourselves, the *experience of body ownership* (EBO) (Seth, 2013) develops early in life, and arises out of the inferential process. Infants watch their hands move across their visual field, integrating exteroceptive visual cues with proprioceptive interoceptive ones to build a sense of "This is *my* hand", in which these "time-locked", one-to-one, self-specifying signals are integrated.

In the "rubber hand illusion" (Botvinick, 2004) the subject experiences a temporary sense of "ownership" of a visible rubber hand if simultaneously stroked in time with his or her concealed actual hand. The brain makes an inferential top-down best guess as to the origin of sensations – "Why on earth would someone be surreptitiously stroking my concealed hand?" – which, in this case erroneously, sets up the illusion of rubber hand ownership in the theatre of consciousness. Again, illusions such as this are curiously entrenched. Even though subjects know at a cortical level that the rubber hand is *not* theirs, they will still flinch when a hammer is threateningly poised above it.

This illusion can be compared with the conviction of worthlessness seen in people suffering from depression, despite abundant evidence to the contrary, or to the feelings of depersonalisation and derealisation which are manifestations of extreme anxiety. Here top-down/bottom-up uncoupling becomes part of pathology. Under conditions of severe pain and/or fear such as childhood sexual abuse, torture, or rape, a protective defensive response is to dissociate into states where one feels "This is not happening to me". Aborting error minimisation means sidestepping the traumatic and unthinkable thought that someone who is supposed to love and protect one is inflicting sadistic fear and pain. This top-down dis-ownership of one's bodily states is protective in the short run, but there may be long-term adverse consequences. The sense of agency may be impaired. In extreme cases the capacity accurately to differentiate between self and other breaks down. A malevolent "alien self" becomes incorporated into a mind, which consequentially feels responsible for its own mental anguish (Fonagy, Gergely, Jurist, & Target, 2002).

The Delphic invocation to "know thyself" is often invoked as a prime aim of psychotherapy. But, deprived of a mirroring, triangulating, a borrowed-brain other, self-knowledge is at best inherently elusive, at worst a narcissistic illusion. Frith (2012, p. 1) cites a range of experimental evidence showing how inaccurate self-appraisal can be, but that "through *discussions of our perceptual experiences with others*, we can detect sensory signals more accurately" (my italics).

Recovery from extreme forms of developmental adversity is not easy. But active inference, if carried out *jointly*, trumps lone attempts to reduce prediction error and therefore helps to minimise free energy and entropic surprise. Therapists help their clients to own their actions, and to become better able to differentiate those for which they are responsible from those in which they were victims, and thus to develop feelings of autonomy and enhanced control over their lives. This means that therapists have, "counter-transferentially", to experience at least an echo of the horrors to which their clients have been subjected. The trauma stories they are called upon to witness will impact on therapists' dynamic unconscious. Feelings of fear, disgust, excitement, and terror are unavoidable. These may fuel acting out on the part of the therapist ("forgetting" sessions, starting late, over-running, or attempts, as Lennon/McCartney put it, to "take their patients home with them"). They can be reassured that these temporary therapeutic mistakes (ruptures) are, if repaired, associated with better therapeutic outcomes, compared with therapists who never transgress or go "off piste" (Safran, 2012). Thus is the dialectic of top-down and bottom-up uncoupling and recoupling built into the everyday rhythms of therapy.

FEP and attachment

We now segue from neuroscience to more familiar psychological and psychotherapeutic territory. Freud started his working life as a neuroanatomist. As early as 1895 he abandoned his attempt to bridge the divide between brain and mind (1940a), moving, as he gave birth to psychoanalysis, to a *psychological* methodology and meta-psychology for probing and understanding the human psyche. His fundamental distinction between conscious and unconscious mental life still stands, although now glossed into the "descriptive unconscious" (the kinds of processes with which the Bayesian approach is concerned) and the "dynamic unconscious", that is, the specific ablation of awareness of painful, conflictual experiences and disruptive impulses.

According to Northoff (2012) the principal reason for Freud's move from brain to mind was that the neuroscience of his day could only describe the brain from the outside, whereas his project was to anatomise the psyche from the inside. Thanks to the advent of brain imaging, the intrinsic life of the brain has become scientifically accessible, prompting the rise of neuropsychoanalysis as a discipline (Panksepp & Solms, 2012). For example, we now know that the brain is energy-hungry, and that it is highly active while seemingly at rest, with the default mode network (DMN) underpinning self-oriented states such as daydreaming and phantasising.

Despite these advances, mind–brain consilience has its limitations. *Pace* Dennett (2017), the "hard problem" will not give up without a fight (Solms, 2019). Experientially at least, mind is not brain, and it is the former with which psychotherapists are concerned. Psychology as an intermediate or transitional zone between brain and behaviour is far from obsolete. We need theories and models of how the mind works – its language, relationships, motivations, desires, plans, and their supporting structures – which are *both* scientifically valid and experience-near.

Here, from a dynamic psychotherapy perspective, Bowlby and Ainsworth's attachment theory stands up as an empirically based psychology which also speaks to the experiential realities of human existence. Birth, love, joy, nurturance, separation, loss, anxiety, bereavement, depression, are all shaped by the attachment dynamic (cf. Holmes & Slade, 2017). Bowlby's project was to bring together systematic observations of parent–offspring interaction with psychoanalytic ideas about the origins of mental pain and the ways that the mind defends itself against disruption. This chapter and the next attempt to link attachment ideas with the FEP neuroscience perspectives we have been considering (cf. Vrticka, 2016).

Attachment theory arose out of John Bowlby's troubled relationship with the psychoanalysis in which he had been trained. Two aspects particularly bothered him. First, the tendency of psychoanalysis of his day (1930s–1960s) to downplay the importance of the environment, past and present, as opposed to unconscious phantasy in shaping psychological distress. Through his work as a child psychiatrist, Bowlby was confronted with poverty, post-war disruption, and psychosocial trauma. Influenced by the new discipline of cybernetics, his thinking was moving towards a systemic and contextual standpoint on psychological life and its vicissitudes. From a Bowlbian perspective, symptoms need to be understood not just intrapsychically, but also in the psychosocial milieu of the family and wider society. The origins of psychopathology lie in the minutiae of parent–child interactions, where psychosocial trauma – death, divorce, separation, abuse, and neglect – leave indelible marks on the developing mind.

Bowlby's second worry was the tendency to view the analyst as "the one who knows", whose interpretations of the unconscious and its hidden meanings were claimed as the curative ingredient. Bowlby, by contrast, saw the principal role of the therapist as providing a *secure base* – a setting in which the patient's distress comes into focus, is given voice, regulated, reflected upon, and in which new meanings spontaneously emerge and begin to be co-constructed.

With a strong academic mind informing his clinical work, Bowlby wanted to find ways to establish psychoanalysis on a firmer scientific footing (Holmes, 2013). He was drawn to ethology, whose pioneers, Konrad Lorenz, Nico Tinbergen, and Robert Hinde used an evolutionary framework to theorise animals' mating and infant-rearing behaviours in the wild. Bowlby realised that comparable systematic "natural" observations could help describe and understand the everyday behaviour of human parents and their offspring. He hoped that this would complement the exclusive focus on phenomena of the consulting room which hitherto had formed the observational base for psychoanalytic theories.

Mary Ainsworth, co-creator of attachment theory, put Bowlby's ideas into observational and experimental practice. She devised a standard test, the "strange situation procedure" (SSP), as a means of studying the attachment dynamic between parents and their one-year-old children. Faced with the threat of a three-minute separation, she and her co-workers found that the dyads fell into a small number of recognisable communicative and behavioural patterns of attachment – secure ("B"), insecure avoidant ("A"), and insecure resistant ("C"). From an FEP perspective these could be thought of as "attractors" which stabilise the complex dynamics of parent–infant interactions. An important finding was that these patterns were specific to mother–infant and father–infant relationships, and thus relatively independent of temperamental or personality variables.

From an FEP perspective, *insecure attachments are vulnerability factors for psychological illness because they compromise active inference* (Holmes & Slade, 2017). In the absence of an external or internal secure base, exploration, physical and psychological, is curtailed. This both limits the extent and range of sensory sampling of the environment, and the variety of priors or hypotheses available to account for them. Both the "breaking" (i.e., creative destruction) of existing priors and the "making" (i.e., creative construction) of new ones are inhibited (Holmes, 2010).

In anxious or "hyperactivating" attachment, agency tends to be absent or eroded. Rather than actively searching or changing their environment, sufferers remain passive in the face of loss, conflict, or trauma (Knox, 2010), a state famously described as "learned helplessness" (Maier & Seligman, 2016). Here the self is suffused with unmodulated affect. In terms of structure learning, commitment to the single prior of *hopelessness* (energy binding, but paralysing) – "Nothing I do will change anything" – precludes finding ways to live productively in the environment in which sufferers find themselves, and inhibits the testing of alternative hypotheses ("Maybe if I try this, things won't be so bad after all").

By contrast, repression, the classical psycho-analytic sense, is the hallmark of deactivating or dismissive attachments. While this yields a measure of niche-specific security, it also renders the individual vulnerable to unexpected trauma or interpersonal friction, as well as, via "toxic stress" (Putnam, Harris, & Putnam, 2013), triggering health-jeopardising physiological changes such as chronic activation of the HPA axis (Dozier, Peloso, Lewis, Laurenceau, & Levine, 2008). One of the functions of negative affect – fear, sadness, mental pain – is as a signal of prediction error. Placing such feelings beyond conscious awareness – beyond mentalising – precludes the learning of more adaptive structural priors.

Disorganised attachment ("D") is a proven precursor to later psychopathology, especially borderline personality disorder (BPD) (Bateman & Fonagy, 2004), and is associated with childhood histories of neglect or abuse. Growing up in an environment where mentalising is absent or impoverished puts these children at risk. Their "hair-trigger" arousal puts them into flight/fight mode, and dissociates cortical modulation of midbrain affect. BPD sufferers typically evince epistemic mistrust or hypervigilance (Fonagy & Allison, 2014), which in turn compromises secure exploration and learning from experience. The "natural pedagogy" (Csriba & Gergely, 2009) – by which parents transmit culture to their offspring – is in question. Establishing the collaborative mentalising duets for one is problematic since their top-down narrative is one in which caregivers, whose borrowed-brain help they might draw on, are the very source of threat or neglect which stimulates the need for PEM. Inhabiting a solipsistic world, deliberate self-harm, substance abuse, or risky sex become self-soothing last resorts. These can be seen in terms of Hopkins's (2016) precision/complexity trade-off. In order to face and make more precise the sensory stimulation association with interpersonal danger, a hand-holding secure base is needed. In their absence, simplistic black/white top-down models prevail.

In all three patterns of insecure attachment,

appropriate complexity is sacrificed for the sake of security. According to Freud (1924e) "neurotics [sic] turn away from reality". From an FEP perspective this can be seen as attempts to minimise free energy, whatever the cost. Fixed beliefs about the world are clung to, rather than updated in the light of experience. The more precision – which may be spurious – is afforded to prior beliefs, the less likely are new experiences sought in order to update generative models. A degree of negative capability, or creative not-knowing, and hence the need for exploration and innovation, is inherent in the free energy formulation, and the probabilistic Bayesian universe. The Kleinian paranoid-schizoid position exemplifies an insecure attachment, complexity-reduced, either/or, good/bad top-down generative model. Attachment security equates to a depressive position world view that offers more complex, nuanced approximations to the world's epistemic affordances.

Therapeutic conversations

"I gotta use words when I talk to you," says T. S. Eliot's (1962) Sweeney. Active inference can be thought of as a dynamic internal conversation, in which extero- and interoceptive sensations are constantly questioned by generative models, and, conversely, in which our models of the world are being iteratively updated in the light of present-moment experience.

This internal conversation, and the "voices" with which it is embodied link with the idea that ultimately, the essence of a psychotherapeutic encounter is *conversation* and *dialogue*, using those terms to cover not just the words which participants use, but also the non-verbal interactions and proto-conversations (including the paradox of communicative silence), by which people engage one another, through gesture, body posture, and tone of voice.

Consider the tennis player John McEnroe's famous challenge to the umpire: "*You cannot be serious*" in calling a ball "out" that the player was convinced was "in". Pre-Hawk-Eye, an FEP-informed umpire might argue:

> "*Neither of us can be absolutely certain whether that ball was on or off the line. Perceptions are inherently subject to error. Tennis balls fly faster than nerve impulses transmit. Your error minimisation procedure is informed by your interoceptive signals of desire to win the match. Your fury is an acting out of that desire, a manifestation of energy unbound. I on the other hand have no vested interest in who wins this game. My error*

minimisation procedure is fuelled neither by amygdala-driven fear of failure, nor wish for dopaminergic reward. The rules of tennis require that you borrow my brain in inherently ambiguous circumstances such as this. My final and considered decision therefore is – the ball was out!"

The word conversation itself, with its implication of both togetherness ("con") and opposition ("versus"), points to the essence of the psychotherapeutic project: acceptance – and challenge. The etymology of the word "conversation" includes the ideas of a) home, and b) sexual intercourse. Both bear on the work of psychotherapy. By providing a "home" – in attachment terms a secure base or holding environment – therapists offer the sense of safety and attention needed to explore and rework one's deepest dispositions. "Sexuality" taken as a metaphor points to the arousal of intersubjectivity, mutuality, complementarity, and somatopsychic excitement which therapy must call into being if more complex psychic structures are to be generated.

If sex is a conversation, and conversation a form of sex, so too is attachment. Although SSP children are mostly pre-verbal, Ainsworth's prototypical attachment patterns, triggered by the parent leaving a one-year-old alone in a strange room for three minutes, can be translated into co-constructed "conversations" on the theme of "danger":

> *"Help, Mum/Dad, where are you? I'm scared. Please come back. Soon. Now."*

> *"It's OK, dearest, I'm here. Big hug. You poor darling, did you think I was gone for ever? I was just in the loo. Everything's alright now. Mummy/Daddy's here. You're all warm and safe and sound. Hey, look at that funny teddy over there."* [Secure]

Or:
> *"Look I'm back now. What was all that fuss about? Do shut up. Wipe away those*

tears. Now let's see if we can make that jigsaw fit together." [Avoidant]

Or:
"Oh dear, do stop crying, you're really upsetting me and all the nice people here. You'll get me crying soon, I can't stand all that racket – you know it gives me a head-ache. And I've got to make a phone call right now. So just stop that noise." [Anx-ious/disorganised]

Tomasello calls these pre-verbal biobe-havioural interactions "proto-conversations", which start in early infancy, and, while constructed from the building blocks of our primate inheri-tance, are specifically human in a number of ways. First, their context is the intensely populated mi-lieu of *collaborative child-rearing* ("It takes a village to raise a child"), unique to our species. Second, proto-conversations depend on *joint attention*, starting from the pointing reflex, in which caregiver and child together focus on an object or situation of interest – that is, affordance – to the participants ("Mum, what's that funny-looking animal?"). In the SSP the focus of attention is the child's distress itself, and what needs to be done about it.

Third, from the caregivers' position, there is a "*We-go*" (as opposed to ego) perspective, in which they put themselves in their infant's shoes (which they may or may not yet be wearing!), thereby creating a reciprocity and a sense of belonging and of "two-getherness". These are all features of the borrowed brain which infants draw on as a reservoir of priors with which to calibrate, articulate, and modulate their affective states.

Fourth, the basics of conversational *turn-taking* are present as the infant "proposes" ("Help") and the parent responds ("Poor you! Is that better now?"). Finally, although much of the conversation is non-verbal, gestural, and physiological (infant heart rate and parent's HPA axis of stress return to baseline as the attachment dynamic is assuaged), *language* accompanies the entire procedure, as parents typically talk their infants through what is happening ("Look, Mummy's back now", etc.). The SSP child is on the threshold of the verbal universe. Parental language reinforces joint attention strategies as it increasingly becomes a shared medium within which a collaborative culture is co-created.

This attempt to translate the proto-conversations of the SSP into spoken language takes us to the attachment dynamic in adults as measured in the "adult attachment interview" (AAI). The AAI was originally devised by Mary Main and her co-workers to reflect the attachment experiences of parents in parallel with their children whom they were studying with the SSP. The AAI rates the *linguistic style* of interviewees as they reflect on their upbringing. This early AAI work was based on the hypothesis that parents' own attachment history will influence the way they handle their children, and thus provide a route for the trans-generational transmission of attachment patterns.

Mary Main had been a student of philosophy

before becoming psychology researcher and was influenced by the Berkeley-based British philosopher, Paul Grice (Duschinsky, 2019). Although the AAI was mainly developed before she made the connection, Main later realised that her categories of linguistic styles paralleled Grice's "maxims" about effective communication: *clarity, relevance, appropriate quality*, and *sufficient quantity*.

AAI categories are based on coding transcripts of individuals' verbal responses to open-ended questions about their parents, early separations, significant losses, and traumata. The originality of the AAI is that it focusses not on the content of respondents' speech, but on its style and structure. It aims to evoke deeper levels of mental function than mere facts, based on the idea that bringing painful and traumatic experience to mind would activate an individual's basic attachment dispositions. To oversimplify, secure individuals' linguistic styles conform to Grice's maxims, while the insecure variants breach them. The resulting categories – secure–autonomous, dismissing, enmeshed/preoccupied, and unresolved – are analogues of the SSP classifications. AAI conversations are thus "back-translated" into the proto-conversations of infancy and early childhood.

An important feature of secure narratives is their "freshness", a feature which Main relates to the fluidity and freedom with which the secure child moves seemingly seamlessly from play, to reassurance, and back again to play, and between the various coordinates of security and interest with which she finds herself. Barratt (2019) contrasts "repetitive-compulsiveness" with the "lifefulness" of psychoanalytic free associative discourse, capturing desire as it erupts into language. An FEP perspective on psychotherapy likewise emphasises the importance of the detail and affective impact of hitherto ignored, repressed, or overridden perceptions and interoceptions. These then present a challenge to find and forge new generative models with which to encompass them.

But prediction error minimisation is never complete or exact. The fountain of free energy always overflows. In the presence of a borrowed brain, including that of a therapist, this stimulates creativity and drives the search for new solutions. When energy minimising is ineffective, as in states of isolation and epistemic hypervigilance, in order to forestall entropic chaos, rigid and simplistic models are adopted, and with them vulnerability to psychological illness.

A shared assumption between the SSP and AAI is that, in both, the attachment dynamic is activated by the procedure itself, and therefore that the resulting behaviours – proximity seeking in the SSP, linguistic styles in the AAI – exemplify in vivo how an individual reacts to stress and threat. However, based on transcript analysis of individual psychotherapy sessions, this has recently been called into question (Talia et al., 2014; Talia, Muzi, Lingiardi, & Taubner, 2018; Talia, Taubner, & Miller-Bottome, 2019). Their analysis arises out of the insight that conversation is not just exchange of information, but consists of interlinked "speech acts" (Austin, 1962) in which the participants try, with varying degrees of success, to influence their interlocutors, control them, shape the prevailing pattern of discourse, achieve emotional proximity or distance, etc.

Talia and colleagues find that the specific *categories of attachment predict how clients speak and manage dialogue in their psychotherapy sessions* (Talia et al., 2014). Secure–autonomous clients' talk is characterised by attentive turn-taking, leading to mutually generated new formulations and solutions to their difficulties. By contrast, dismissive individuals' dialogue resists new perspectives, downplaying or retracting emerging emotions and efforts at restructuring. Anxiously attached clients tend to spin confusing monologues in which therapists find it difficult to find, engage or initiate reciprocal dialogue.

The course of true therapy never runs smooth. The majority of patients coming for help will manifest various forms of insecure attachment. From an FEP perspective, insecure dialogic styles reflect a top-down strategy in which the need for a modicum of security restricts exploration and innovation. Therapeutic skill depends on being able to turn the impasse created by these insecure dialogic patterns into a conversational focus. Therapists enjoin clients to "mentalise" what is happening between them:

> *"I get the feeling you're pretty unimpressed with this therapy so far. Maybe you think I'm just trotting out old psychobabble, and don't really understand how desperate you are for a lifeline and for someone to suggest what you can do about everything horrible that is going on."*

> *"Did you notice that our conversations tend to take a step forward and then immediately backtrack. You started to say how frightened you felt as a child when left alone while your Mom was working, but then immediately let her off the hook: 'Hey! there are hundreds of latchkey kids, so what am I making such a fuss about?'"*

"Sometimes it seems it's difficult for you to imagine I can hold you in mind, not just between sessions, but even as we are talking. It's as though you need to keep my attention at all times, otherwise you imagine I'll drift off into thinking about other things, rather as your parents were in such a dope-filled haze that they were barely aware of you children."

WHAT IS THE AAI MEASURING?

In contrast to Main's assumption, Talia's group found that *speech act analysis held true across all conversational topics, even if they did not represent threat* and therefore were unlikely to be activating the attachment dynamic. But if the AAI is not measuring an individual's attachment disposition, what psychological phenomenon is it tapping into? To discuss this we must, as Talia, Taubner, and Miller-Bottome (2019) suggest, step back to Bowlby – and sideways to Grice's successors, Wilson and Sperber (2002).

Bowlby's thinking was shaped by two

self-imposed restraints, both of which can now be called into question. First, he never deviated from the idea that our attachment life was to be understood in terms of the "environment of evolutionary adaptedness" (EEA) in which our ancestors emerged, and where *protection from predation* was the driver leading to the evolution of the attachment dynamic. Given the comparative safety – some would say excessive safety – of modern child-rearing environments, this appears to be only part of the story. Alongside response to threat, "attachment" is now thought to subsume other interpersonal developmental processes, especially the affect co-regulation and parental pedagogy underpinning epistemic trust (Holmes & Slade, 2017). If this is valid, the AAI as measuring stick elicits interviewees' basic interpersonal dispositions, especially their presumptions about intimate others' trustworthiness and their capacity to help co-regulate feelings.

From an FEP perspective this suggests that the AAI taps into a person's readiness to borrow another's brain so that, with the help of a caregiver's top-down priors, pain and uncertainty can be managed. Insecure attachments reflect ways of adapting to suboptimal collaboration. If the other is felt to be controlling or invasive, then a rebuffing style may typify his or her conversational patterns. Seeing dialogue in terms of interactive *speech acts* rather than information exchange reveals how language is used to manage feelings – pulling the interlocutor in, keeping her at bay, blocking him, etc.

Bowlby's second principle was that in studying the effects of developmental adversity he should confine himself to objectively observable events such as parental death, illness, or divorce, or to specific explicitly stated threats. He fully understood the importance of procedural rather than episodic aspects of the developmental process such as parental mal-handling, neglect, and the overall family milieu, but thought that these were too difficult to measure, and that attempts to do so would weaken his argument, especially with a hos-

tile psychoanalytic community. This meant that
the unconscious aspects of developmental psychology, in contrast to the explicit and externally
observable, were downplayed in the evolution of
attachment theory (Duschinsky, 2019). Seeing
the AAI in terms of threat was consistent with this,
and reflected Main's loyalty to Bowlby's vision.
Going beyond these self-imposed limitations, we
can now see how a person's conversational style
both reveals and conceals the contours of their
inner world as they engage with others.

THE RELEVANCE OF RELEVANCE

This takes us to "relevance theory", an updated
version of "Grice's maxims" (Wilson & Sperber,
2002). Relevance theory is based on a number of
ideas. First, it asserts that communication is *ostensive*: out of all possible stimuli, it *points* to something
that is of importance, interest, or relevance – provides affordance – to the interlocutor(s). Second,
communication is always *contextual*, that is, arising

out of the situation in which the participants find themselves. Let's imagine someone says "I'm going to the bank". Whether they are carrying a fishing rod or a wallet will immediately indicate which sort of "bank" they mean. Third, communication is *fast and frugal*, in that both communicator and listener use minimum effort for their verbal exchanges. This means that listening is largely "inferential" – in FEP terms "actively inferential" – in the sense that the Bayesian listener *predicts* the likely meaning of the message as much from its implications as from the words themselves, which are often vague and imprecise ("ah-ha ... y'know what I mean ..." etc.).

Relevance theory is applicable to psychotherapy in a number of ways. First, ostensive communication takes us back to the idea of *joint attention*, pointing to a topic on which client and therapist mutually focus: initially the "presenting problem" which brings the client for help, or, as therapy proceeds, an unmodulated affect which unexpectedly overwhelms the client, or the interactional patterns arising between them. The therapist's role is to help maintain focus on "the subject", while temporarily going along with and tracking the client's deviations or distractions.

The notion of *context* is equally of great relevance to psychoanalytic psychotherapy. Topics of conversation in the consulting room – beyond their arbitrary, literal, or conventional reference – are typically thought of as referring indirectly to the therapeutic relationship itself. Hence the generally accepted therapeutic trope that if a client talks, say, about the untrustworthiness of political leaders, she might indirectly be referring to an upcoming break and the impact this will have on her sense of being able to trust her therapist.

This contextual aspect is especially important when considering unintended, unconscious, or unintegrated aspects of clients' mental life. The therapist's top-down store of experience, narrative envelopes, and imagery is drawn on in order to find the psychic relevance of the conversational topic. The highest levels of generative models are inherently multivalent. Comparably, Freud's "switch words" (Freud, 1900a; Litowitz, 2014) are linguistic nodal points where conscious and unconscious themes coincide, and where meanings can branch off in a number of directions. Sensitive to the polysematism of language, therapists are always on the lookout for self-salient themes embedded in their clients' speech.

Let's return to our example. The client apologises for being slightly late as she "had to go to the bank, and there was a queue". The therapist might pick up on this "cue", suggesting that perhaps she was anxious because she could not "bank" on his support, especially during a holiday absence. The FEP resonance here is that the higher one goes up the inferential error-minimising hierarchy, the more general, non-specific, and multi-contextual priors become. The words "bank" and queue/cue are applicable to a variety of contexts, conscious and unconscious. The psychotherapist's task is to find an interpersonal, often unconscious, and warded-off contextual relevance for their clients' utterances.

This takes us back to the AAI, the four pro-

totypical conversational patterns it delineates, and
their relevance to psychotherapy. All can be seen
in terms of "natural pedagogy", and the varieties
of epistemic trust or mistrust (Csibra & Gergely,
2009) that prevail in an individual's developmental history. The secure, fluid/autonomous style
characterises the kinds of conversations therapists
would hope to generate with their clients, fulfill-
ing Grice's maxims, and those of relevance theory.
It implies joint attention to a mutually identified
topic in which the client senses the therapist's
exclusive and undistracted focus on his inner
and outer worlds, and where multiple contexts,
conscious and unconscious, are held in play. The
"fast and frugal" aspect captures the relaxed and
frequently enjoyable sense of mutual comprehension that often feels "beyond words" in which the
client feels "understood", while at the same time
this inferential comprehension is always subject
to error and correction.

By contrast, insecure patterns on the AAI fall
into three types: dismissive, enmeshed, and inco-

herent. Dismissive talk points fleetingly and then withdraws, fearing change and its consequences, then resisting elaboration or exploration:

> *"I had an awful time at work yesterday … but that's normal isn't it, everyone has bad days."*

> *"Yeah, I was bullied a lot at school, but, so what, that's past history now …"*

Enmeshed talk obfuscates contextualisation, drawing the listener into a confusing maze of past and present, making it hard to find a point of joint attention where therapist and patient can come together at the same time and in the same conversational place.

> *"Mother was all over the place … she is now … I was a frightened child … I don't know what to do … I ought to go and see her but … you know … she never answers*

the phone … it's so hard … but who does these days … it's all mobiles …"

In disorganised/incoherent talk there are sudden fractures in narrative coherence and sequence, often leaving the listener unable to follow, forced to fill in the gaps based on her countertransference, but feeling it might not be safe to probe further.

"I saw a dog run over in the road as I was coming today … that's why I'm late …. War's a terrible thing…. I'm back on drugs you know …"

Helping clients to move from these defensive patterns towards more secure and salutary talk is the central business of psychotherapy, and constitutive of psychotherapy competence. In the final chapters I turn to the implications of how FEP can both inform practice, and provide an overall scientific framework for the psychotherapeutic project.

8

Practical implications for psychotherapists

Planets revolve around suns, and apples fall from
trees without asking permission from Newton's
laws of gravity. Minds continue to love and hate,
come together and fall apart happily or unhappily,
oblivious to the brain mechanisms which shape
their motions. To put it another way – does any of
this FEP business matter? For the jobbing psychotherapist, does the FEP framework amount to any
more than Molière's gentleman's discovery that he
has been speaking "prose" all his life? The focus
of this final chapter is to examine what sort of dif-
ference the new neurobiology, important though

it may be, might make to psychotherapists as they go about their daily work.

"PLAIN OLD THERAPY" (CF. ALLEN, 2012)

The Helmholtzian model of the brain depicts a series of nested Markov blankets, increasing in generality and abstraction as they ascend towards consciousness. There is "conversation" at all levels between the sensorium, external and internal, and top-down models. The driver for these conversations is the need for error minimisation – ever attempting to align generative models with incoming information about the world and its affordances, external and internal.

Psychotherapy in its various guises engages with these processes in a number of ways. Free association reduces error vis-à-vis the external and internal world by focussing on and augmenting the bottom-up "granularity" of experience. It improves the precision we need to find ways to be better adapted to our selves, our intimate others, and our interactions with them. At the other end of the prediction error minimising (PEM) process, the borrowed brain of the therapist offers an extended range of narratives – "interpretations" – of the self and its relationships, again minimising error with the help of this extended repertoire. The emotional engagement of patient and therapist, manifest in transference, means that errors can and will be acted out, worked and lived through, and so "minimised", in vivo, but relatively harmlessly. Mentalising, thinking about thinking, puts a brake on the automatic, anachronistic, complexity-degraded processes of error minimisation, enabling both bottom-up sensations and top-down models to be scrutinised, augmented, and better aligned. Let's now revisit some of the themes we have surveyed in earlier chapters.

ACTION AND AGENCY

Action is the prime means for improving the precision of sensory sampling and thus minimising prediction error. That rather abstract statement forms the basis of much of the rationale for cognitive behavioural therapy (CBT). Clients suffering from depression are conceptualised as being in the thrall of cognitive errors which dominate their affective world: "Everyone hates me", "I am useless", etc. These self-perpetuating, albeit spuriously parsimonious generalisations bind free energy, but also undermine agency. Passive helplessness pervades, interspersed with self-perpetuating depressive auto-denigration. CBT encourages its clients to see these negative views as "hypotheses", in need of active testing through "experiments". Action is thereby encouraged, with the hand-holding help of a therapist, enhancing sensory precision and reducing prediction error. When things go well, depressive priors begin to be revised in the light of experience: "Maybe I'm not such a failure as I thought I was".

In psychoanalytic therapies the role of "action" is less explicit. But the very act of seeking help for psychological difficulties implies a degree of agency. Moreover, the process of "giving sorrow words" in the therapeutic setting, if seen in terms of speech acts, is agency-enhancing. By helping clients find the words to actualise their inchoate feelings, therapists help with the error minimisation that is, in Bernard's terms, the condition of a free life. Expressing negative affect, with its concomitant enhancement of attention to interceptive detail, is especially conducive to reworking dysfunctional priors.

Action modifies input so that discrepancies between the world we find ourselves in, and our models of that world, are less at loggerheads. We flock with like-minded birds and, via projective identification, may induce our intimates to reinforce our oversimplified expectations. This minimises error and binds free energy, and in the short run is adaptive, but also forestalls salutary model modification and enhancing complexity. The inherent "uncoupling"/virtual reality nature of psychotherapy aims to help clients catch themselves as they try unconsciously to bend their environment, typically through transferential assumptions about the therapist, to pre-existing pathogenic models of the world.

Therapy works with this to help clients act more freely, rather than being condemned to repeat a past which, sequestered from PEM, has been inaccessible to model revision.

DUETS FOR ONE

As biobehavioural synchrony embeds itself, clients become more adventurous, knowing that their hand is being metaphorically held, and that energy binding can be temporarily left to the therapist. In these "duet for one" moments, initially fleetingly, therapist and client sing joint songs, belonging both to each and neither participant. The absence of face-to-face contact of classical analytic topography may encourage this. The prone client can temporarily take his analyst as part of himself, relying on her professional energy-binding skills, and so feel safer to imagine alternative voices, scenarios, and futures.

Competent therapists are flexible, sensitive, and responsive. They are tuned in to the moment-to-moment actuality of their clients' inner lives, while at the same time encompassing an over-all model of the mind and how its distress might be alleviated (Lemma, Target, & Fonagy, 2008). Many therapeutic conversations have this "duet for one" quality, in which therapists maintain a fragile synthesis through scrupulous attention to and use of the client's linguistic and psychosocial universe. Adopting the Friston and Frith (2015) model, listener's and speaker's brain/minds over-lap, creating a temporary "group mind". Thoughts and sensations are, for the moment, jointly owned. The patient's free associations and therapist's countertransference feelings bring interoceptive input into the arena. The top-down models these stimulate in the therapist's mind are offered to the client in the service of error minimisation.

LANGUAGE

The previous chapter explored the role of interac-tive speech patterns in client and therapist from an attachment viewpoint. Thus far, the FEP research literature has had little to say directly about language. But first principles would suggest its vital importance at the upper reaches of the PEM hierarchy. The environment stimulates sensations on a continuous spectrum, whether of wavelength, intensity, or frequency. Interoceptive receptors likewise are graded rather than digitalised. Top-down sensations are classified into discrete units of sound and colour.

As anyone attempting to learn a "foreign" language as an adult knows, this applies especially to speech. The sounds speakers emit are continuous, but as we gradually become familiar with the language, syllables and words begin to emerge as identifiable entities. Language was a massive step-change in human evolution for two main reasons. First, with its help, perceptions become "fast and frugal". Returning to the Chapter 2 example, the words "bird" or "plastic" captured, with minimum cerebral energy expenditure, the relevant information about a salient experience. Second, language provides the essential medium for brain-borrowing and duets for one. Language ensures that when you say "cat" I can reliably assume we are both referring to the same quadrupedal long-tailed feline. Ironically, when things go wrong, the integrative pull-together power of language reveals itself all the more:

> *You say eether and I say eyether*
> *You say neether and I say nyther*
> *Eether, eyether, neether, nyther*
> *Let's call the whole thing off!*
> (George & Ira Gershwin, 1937, "Let's call the whole thing off")

To recall an incident from the author's training, he was observing a young woman with anorexia nervosa being interviewed by a senior psychiatrist. In an interchange that lasted for five minutes or more, the following interchange was repeated over and over:

> *Interviewer: "Do you worry about your appearance?"*

Patient: "Oh, no they're fine, I never think about my parents" … etc., etc.

Thus do we learn more from our mistakes than our successes – for psychiatrists a reassuring thought!

Language conceals and reveals in equal measure. While English speakers say "blue", Russian speakers will ask which of the two blues their language provides is meant. When a patient says she's suffering from "depression", therapists will want to know what she "means", what the depression is "like", where it hurts in her body, what thoughts it evokes, and how it affects her life. Therapeutic conversations insert a wedge into everyday PEM where bottom-up and top-down collide or collude seemingly seamlessly. Uncoupling pushes down into the granularity of experience, and upward towards a mentalising stance.

Effective therapists need to develop "perfect pitch" for the nuances of language and how it is spoken. They are careful to adjust their speech to the specific verbal repertoire of the client. The two components of effective therapy, empathy and challenge, depend on contrasting linguistic modes. Sound recordings reveal that empathic resonance on the part of the therapist stays within the confines of the patient's speech style, range of reference, and vocal pitch; thus is duet-for-one ambience preserved (Avdi & Seikkula, 2019). When therapists switch to challenge or "interpretation", their voice rises in pitch and volume, thereby reflecting a "higher" level of the PEM hierarchy.

The "conversational model" or "psychodynamic interpersonal therapy" (PIT) (Barkham, Guthrie, Hardy, & Margison, 2017) specifically foregrounds the therapeutic role of dialogue strategies. A prime therapeutic aim is to help clients develop a "feeling language" with which to give form to their inchoate sufferings. In the course of treatment patients learn to listen to their bodily sensations, and to find words with which to express, manage, and live with them. This corresponds with helping to overcome the interoception/generative model deficit, especially found in avoidant clients. Attention to the "minute particulars" of experience is emphasised, especially insofar as they are salient to the specific affordances of an individual's life. As Clark (2016, p. 195) puts it, these consist of

> ... world[s] parsed according to our organ-ism-specific needs and action repertoire ... populated with items such as hidden but tasty prey, poker hands, handwritten digits, and structured meaningful sentences ...

PIT also emphasises the role of one's inner voice(s), originating in mother–infant conversations, verbal and non-verbal, elaborated into inner "I-Me" self-speech typically seen (and heard) in three- to four-year-old children. Their play is accompanied by a "running commentary" which by five years has been mostly internalised. In therapy it is once more externalised as the client speaks herself "out loud" in the attentive listening presence of the therapist (cf. Meares, 2005).

SURPRISE

An important psychotherapeutic implication of FEP is that in its mission to minimise surprise, as a proxy for entropy or free energy, the brain/mind can diminish or obliterate complexity and differentiation. The relational bedrock of psychotherapy helps clients tolerate and survive *surprise*, and so find new and more healthy ways of binding mental energy.

Validation, empathy, and radical acceptance (Holmes & Slade, 2017) are preconditions for the establishment of duets for one. But the other half of the therapeutic dialectic is challenge and radical *non*-acceptance of self-destructive, self-immiserating, restrictive psychological formations. By mirroring and role-responsiveness, the analyst enters into patients' "idiolect", a person's unique way of seeing the world and self-stamped vernacular. At this stage, from the patient's point of view, the top-down/bottom-up process runs smoothly, avoiding any great anomalies or surprises.

But, at some point, a discrepancy will inevitably arise. The analyst, in her chosen role of
anonymity and ambiguity, will fail to conform to
the patient's top-down expectations. In Strachey's
(1934) account, the feared superego father turns
out to be relatively benign. Today (cf. Lear, 2011) a
patient's view of her analyst as abusive ("*You're just
getting off on my misery; you don't really give a damn*")
might be confounded by compassionate and com-
mitted concern. Conversely, patients' hopes that
their therapists will be all-loving or all-forgiving
may come up against tough comments, requests
for payment and punctual but abrupt endings to
sessions. This therapeutic ambiguity now puts
patients (which of course include, through their
personal therapy, analysts themselves) in a "benign
bind". They need and want to remain in the therapeutic relationship, but since old models no longer
work to minimise free energy, psychic reorgani-
sation is triggered, with its associated short-term
(hopefully) confusion and mental pain.

It is no mean task for analysts to challenge

their patients, to break the mould of maladaptive energy binding, and to move psychic structures towards greater complexity. It is tempting to collude by "supportively" maintaining the status quo, or gratefully accepting a "difficult" patient's dropout. But the purpose of the therapy is to generate, tolerate, bind, and metabolise novelty and surprise. The chaos-theory chemist Prigogine (1980) argues that the emergence of molecular complexity requires the combination of a closed system and raised temperature and pressure. Analogously, the holding function of a therapeutic relationship in which neither analyst nor patient allow themselves to escape, physically or mentally, forms the crucible, or "closed system", in which more adaptive and complex generative models can be forged.

CREATIVITY

FEP emphasises conservation and surprise minimisation, as at first sight does attachment theory with its foregrounding of the security imperative. But we've seen how a feature of secure–autonomous dialogue in the AAI is its freshness and spontaneity. Psychological health entails exploration, innovation, and creativity.

The healthy brain is a virtual reality generator, able to dream, imagine and fantasise. This takes us back to Helmholtz, and his advocacy of science as opposed to the prevailing culture of German romanticism. Coleridge, another polymath and multilinguist (R. Holmes, 1989), was responsible for bringing Goethe and his colleagues into the anglophone world. This is his famous account of the workings of the imagination:

> *Most of my readers will have observed a small water-insect on the surface of rivulets … and will have noticed, how the little animal wins its way up against the stream, by alternate pulses of active and passive motion, now resisting the current, and now yielding to it in order to gather strength and a momentary fulcrum for a further propulsion.*

This is no unapt emblem of the mind's self-experience in the act of thinking. There are evidently two powers at work, which relatively to each other are active and passive; and this is not possible without an intermediate faculty, which is at once both active and passive ... we must denominate this intermediate faculty ... the IMAGI-NATION. (1817, p. 203)

Coleridge's dialectic of spontaneity and control, activity and passivity, is not far removed from Helmholtzian top-down/bottom-up processes. Sensations are received relatively passively; they are then actively shaped by top-down processes. Their error-minimising meeting points – occurring at several nested Markov blanket stages between sense organs and consciousness – form the cambium for innovation and creativity. With the *default mode network* activated, new ideas, arising out of dreams and free associations, emerge as one passively "listens to oneself" and at the same time, actively "listens to oneself listening". When the need for sheer survival has ousted the capacity for creative living, the "absence/presence" (Barratt, 2019) of a therapist becomes the vital ingredient in revivifying this process.

EPILOGUE

As we move towards an ending, I hope I have communicated my enthusiasm for FEP as a new paradigm that can help validate and advance aspects of psychoanalytic theory and practice, and psychotherapy generally. My reservations have been muted and minimal. But FEP has not received universal acceptance. Its status is still debatable, having been described as an unfalsifiable platitude, an imperative, a tautology, a stipulative definition, paradigm, law of the life sciences, law of nature, an a priori first principle, a unifying explanation, and a simple postulate or axiom (Colombo & Wright, 2018).

From a mathematical neuroscience point of view, its very general applicability makes it hard to specify what might or might not constitute a testable and scientifically validating refutation (Tozzi & Peters, 2017). Rather as in fundamental physics, string theory is (I am told!) intellectually and mathematically satisfying, but remains in the realm of theoretical speculation, so FEP is an exciting and wide-ranging guiding "principle" or heuristic, but currently without overwhelming empirical support.

From a psychoanalytic angle, Blass and Carmeli (2007, 2015) have strongly disputed Yovell, Solms, and Fotopoulou's (2015) assertion that neuropsychoanalysis enhances psychotherapeutic understanding and practice. Philosophically the easy use of the mind/brain trope, or dual aspect monism, leaves the "hard problem" untouched (cf. Dennett, 2017; Solms, 2019). The "is-ness" of experience, especially those with which psychotherapy deals – love, loss, pain, hope – seem to inhabit a different realm to the mathematics of surprise.

I end by reiterating my enthusiasm, based on four main themes. First, FEP is a dynamic theory, visualising continuous interplay between the mind and its environment, internal and external. Instead of "the unconscious" as a reified entity, FEP

Epilogue

depicts interactive interplay between unconscious and conscious parts of the mind as desires and security-seeking struggle for satisfaction in an entropic world. Second, once the "duet for one"/borrowed-brain element is included in FEP it speaks directly to the interpersonal attachment-based strand of psychoanalytic psychotherapy. Third, with its Bayesian roots, FEP puts uncertainty and the need for prediction at the heart of its theory, and this chimes with the psychoanalytic valuation of not-knowing and respect for experiential mystery. Fourth, FEP celebrates the creative, innovative and imaginative aspect of the brain as it generates dreams and narratives as top-down ingredients in the PEM process.

My enthusiasm for FEP also comes from the meta-perspective of psychotherapy integration (cf. Holmes & Bateman, 2002). This holds that the mutative aspects of psychotherapy derive largely from common factors, encompassing the therapeutic relationship itself, a consistent theoretical framework, and change-promoting procedures

(Holmes & Slade, 2017). FEP provides a meta-meta-perspective on this common factors approach (Wampold, 2015). If psychological health is associated with binding free energy and minimising prediction error, then procedures which foster these will be likely to be helpful, whatever their espoused brand name. These include: liberating agency; enhancing sensory sampling whether through CBT "experiments" or psychoanalytic free association; widening the range of possible top-down hypotheses through dream analysis and interpretation and the "active imagination"; fostering change-precipitating sadness; and modifying priors in the light of experience.

These require a context of biobehavioural synchrony, epistemic trust, and conversational turn-taking, duet-for-one dialogue. From a research perspective these features are benchmarks for assessing psychotherapy efficacy and compliance. Clinically they help concentrate therapists' and their supervisors' minds, and improve outcomes.

A final point is that FEP suggests psychotherapy, rather than being an esoteric concoction,
exemplifies a "natural kind", a specialised form of
a more general cultural phenomenon, increasingly needed in rapidly changing and unpredictable
environments. Many aspects of cultural life – play,
sport, drama, iconography – depend on the top-
down/bottom-up "uncoupling" together with
meta-cognition which fosters health-promoting
PEM. A Shakespeare play or a rock concert lib-
erate erotic and destructive energies, but, at the
end of the performance, no one has been hurt or
abused (one hopes), as the performers' bows and
audiences' applause acknowledge.

The psychological homeostasis essential to
free life is inherently vulnerable to the forces of entropy. Learning to experience, tolerate, and resolve
prediction error depends largely on the generative
possibilities of intimate relationships. Societies
that engender anxiety, passivity, inequality, isolation, and insecurity compromise the development
of the capacity for this free energy binding in the

developing child. In the long run only social change will shift this self-inflicted culture of immiseration. But alongside this, where spontaneous self-correction has failed or faltered, psychotherapy, combined with other cultural aspects of the "psychological immune system" (Holmes, 2014), offers a route – albeit one not without its perils – to new hopes and horizons.

GLOSSARY OF TERMS

ACTIVE INFERENCE (AI)

AI is the prime means by which the brain makes sense of the world in which it finds itself. It assumes the brain is an inference machine that approximates optimal probabilistic (Bayesian) belief updating. The AI brain embodies an internal model of the world and itself that simulates the bottom-up sensory data that it should receive if its top-down model of the world is correct. These predicted sensory data are then compared to actual observations. Deviations between predicted and observed sensations are used – prior to post – to update the model.

ADULT ATTACHMENT INTERVIEW (AAI)

An hour-long open-ended interview in which clients' experiences of loss, separation trauma, and neglect are explored. Transcripts are analysed for their linguistic styles and classified as secure–autonomous, insecure–dismissive, insecure–enmeshed, and unresolved.

AFFORDANCE

An organism's affordances are the specific aspects of its environment which are salient to its survival, and to which it must attend: food, predators, habitat niche (which in our species mainly means fellow humans).

ATTRACTORS

Attractors are islands of stability in a sea of chaos. Dynamic complex systems are inherently chaotic and unstable, but they usually settle down into one of a number of possible steady states, or "attractor basins".

BAYESIAN BRAIN

Brains make "educated guesses" about their future, short- and long-term: what to expect from the environment, and how the organism itself will respond. These predictions are probabilistic and depend on real-time approximations to guide actions and homeostatic responses to ever-changing conditions.

BOTTOM-UP/TOP-DOWN
The neural patterns stimulated by the impact of the environment, exteroceptive and interoceptive and proprioceptive, travel "bottom upwards" towards the cerebral cortex where they encounter patterns based on preformed generative models travelling in the opposite direction, "top downwards".

COGNITIVE BEHAVIOURAL THERAPY (CBT)
A therapy which challenges the faulty cognitive constructs theorised to underlie psychological illness. CBT encourages clients to conduct "experiments" in which these beliefs are put to the test and to accept the verdict of reality if they are refuted. From a PEM perspective CBT fosters action, and generative model revision.

DEFAULT MODE NETWORK (DMN)

The brain continues to be energetically active when in a resting state and not attending to specific tasks. The DMN is a connected network of regions of the brain, including the medial prefrontal cortex (MPFC), activated when daydreaming or thinking about oneself and one's history, recent and past, and in relation to others. From an FEP perspective the DMN can be thought of as a reservoir of generative models of self–other interactions.

ENTROPY

A measure of the disorder of a system. Originally defined in relation to thermodynamic systems it reflects the surplus randomness that is unavailable for work. In mind/brain terms this translates to Freud's "energy unbound" that threatens to disrupt adaptive processes. The second law of thermodynamics states that the entropy of a system never decreases over time. The universe as whole is cooling and tending towards disorder, while life, in a purely local sense, resists this tendency.

FREE ENERGY PRINCIPLE (FEP)
Biological agents counteract disorder and therefore must minimise the entropy of their sensory states. Energy unbound is entropic, that is, it spells disorder/chaos. The brain "binds" incoming informational energy according to its predictive models of the world. This means the agents limiting themselves to a small number of possible states of brain/mind.

GENERATIVE MODELS
Generative models are the predictive models which the brain uses to account for the causes of its sensations. Generative models inform active inference, which confirms or disconfirms beliefs about the world and modifies them in the light of experience. Generative models translate psychoanalytically as internal working models, object relations, and transferential assumptions.

GRANULARITY
Sensations, whether internal or external, can be vague ("vagal" = the wandering tenth cranial nerve),

brushed aside altogether, or highly specific. The more "granular" the more detailed and affectively informative. Although from different psychotherapy traditions, both free association and mindfulness encourage subjects to increase their receptiveness to the "pixelation" or granularity of experience.

HYPOTHALAMIC-PITUITARY-ADRENAL AXIS (HPA)

The link between the hormonal and the central nervous systems (CNS). The HPA axis is a self-regulating assembly of endocrine glands that control and secrete adrenaline, cortisol, and other hormones that help respond to stressful events. "Toxic stress" reflects chronic hyperactivity of the HPA axis and has long-term negative consequences for physical and mental health.

INTEROCEPTION

The sensations provided from within the body as opposed to the external environment – feelings in the gut, genitals, chest, skin, limbs, etc. Many of these are transmitted to the brain via the vagus nerve.

"Polyvagal theory" emphasises the importance of interoceptions as underpinning the affective life of especial interest to psychotherapists.

MARKOV BLANKETS

These are the interface points between bottom-up input and top-down inferences. Everything we know about the world comes ultimately from our senses – our own and those transmitted by our intimates and the prevailing culture. A Markov blanket is a statistical boundary that makes these bottom-up and top-down variables independent, and in need of active inference attempting to align one with the other. Markov blankets apply at the level of the sense organs, but also within a neural hierarchy in which each level of upward information is "questioned" by downstream generative models.

MENTALISING

Is to have the insight that we see the world through a veil of thought or "theory of mind", and to appreciate that others also have their own unique desires, perspectives, projects, and concepts. To mentalise is to see oneself from the outside and others from the inside.

NEGENTROPY

The order, structure, and complexity which characterises life, in contrast to the molecular simplicity, randomness, and cooling over time which characterises inanimate matter.

PREDICTION ERROR MINIMISATION (PEM)

Accurate perception necessitates optimising the precision of top-down priors and bottom-up sensory evidence. Neurobiologically, this corresponds to modulating the "gain" of error-units. Given the discrepancy between input, and models to account for it, the brain minimises error in two ways: a) through action, whereby the accuracy of the input can be modified ("Let's look a little closer"), and b) by model revision ("Maybe I was wrong. Did you hear a noise? – perhaps it was just the wind").

PRIORS AND POSTERIORS

Priors are the generative models one brings to bear on sensory experience, assumptions, and preconceptions. Posteriors are the newly revised models once active inference has been applied.

PROJECTIVE IDENTIFICATION (PI)

A concept originally developed by Melanie Klein in which an infant projects difficult or unwanted affects into a primary caregiver, whose role is to "metabolise" these and to return them to the child in manageable form. The concept was extended by Bion to describe non-verbal forms of communication and affective empathy. PI is a feature of emotional communication in psychotherapy, especially when working with traumatised clients. In FEP it relates to the idea of "niche construction" in which we create the world in accordance with our generative models.

PSYCHOANALYTIC PSYCHOTHERAPY

One to three times a week therapy following psychoanalytic techniques and theories, including clearly time-bounded sessions, relative therapist opacity, free association, dream analysis, interpreting transference, and drawing on therapist's countertransference to understand client's emotional states.

STRANGE SITUATION

A standardised method of measuring the attachment status of one- to two-year-old children and their parents. After an initial period of relaxed play, the child is subjected to a series of mild stresses as the parent goes out of the room for three minutes. Video analysis of how parent and child handle this separation and reunion leads to a classification of secure, insecure–avoidant, –anxious, or –disorganised attachments.

SURPRISE

An everyday word with a technical meaning: mathematically the negative log probability of an outcome. Surprise is the discrepancy between input information ("recognition density") and prior expectations. It is a measure of how unexpected a sensation/experience is, and carries a high degree of information and potential free energy. The brain aims to minimise surprise by reducing ambiguity through action and by modifying priors. Mathematically, free energy is always greater than surprise, so minimising surprise will likewise tame free energy.

ACKNOWLEDGEMENTS

Many of the ideas in this book began life as conversations with family, friends, colleagues, and students, and in lectures, including those arranged by Confer before they embarked on this innovative publishing project. I am grateful to Evrinomy Avdi, Peter Fonagy, Karl Friston, Josh Holmes, Lydia Holmes, Matt Holmes, Ros Holmes, Jim Hopkins, Richard Mizen, Nick Sarra, Alessandro Talia, and Kristin White for their contributions, reactions, corrections, and amplifications. Especial thanks go to Jacob Holmes who made a major contribution to Chapter 1; to Arietta Slade and Tobias Nolte with whom many of these ideas were first forged; and to Patrick Connolly and Michael Moutoussis who generously gave up their time to read the entire text. All have made invaluable suggestions. If in this "borrowed brain" collage they recognise their ideas, even if somewhat mangled, I hope they will take this as sincere homage. I own up to mistakes, misunderstandings, oversimplifications, anachronisms, and all other horrible and probable howlers.

Earlier versions of some of the material here appeared in Holmes and Slade (2017) and Holmes and Nolte (2019).

REFERENCES

Allen, B., Bendixsen, B., Fenerci, R. B., & Green, J. (2018). Assessing disorganized attachment representations: a systematic psychometric review and meta-analysis of the Manchester Child Attachment Story Task. *Attachment & Human Development*. doi: 10.1080/14616734.2018.1429477

Allen, J. G. (2012). *Restoring Mentalizing in Attachment Relationships: Treating Trauma with Plain Old Therapy*. New York: American Psychiatric Association Publishing.

Allen, J. G., Fonagy, P., & Bateman, A. (2008). *Handbook of Mentalizing in Mental Health Practice*. Arlington, VA: American Psychiatric Association Publishing.

Austin, J. (1962). *How to Do Things with Words*. Oxford: Oxford University Press.

Avdi, E., & Seikkula, J. (2019). Studying the process of psychoanalytic psychotherapy: discursive and embodied aspects. *British Journal of Psychotherapy*, 35: 217–232.

Badcock, P., Davey, C., Whittle, S., Allen, N., & Friston, K. J. (2017). The depressed brain: an evolutionary systems theory. *Trends in Cognitive Sciences*, 21: 182–194. doi: /10.1016/j. tics.2017.01.005

Badcock, P., Friston, K. J., Maxwell, J., & Ramstead, J. (2019). The hierarchically mechanistic mind: a free-energy formulation of the human psyche. *Physics of Life Reviews*. doi: 10.1016/j. plrev.2318.10.002

Barkham, M., Guthrie, E., Hardy, G., & Margison, F. (2017). *Psychodynamic-interpersonal Therapy: a Conversational Model*. London: SAGE.

Barratt, B. (2016). *Radical Psychoanalysis*. London: Routledge.

Barratt, B. (2019). *Beyond Psychotherapy*. London: Routledge.

Barrett, L. (2017). *How Emotions Are Made*. London: Pan.

Bateman, A., & Fonagy, P. (2004). *Psychotherapy for Borderline*

Personality Disorder: Mentalization-based Treatment. New York: Oxford University Press.

Belloc, H. (1907). *Cautionary Tales for Children*. London: Blackwood.

Belsky, J., Bakermans-Kranenburg, M. J., & van Ijzendoorn, M. H. (2007). For better and for worse: Differential susceptibility to environmental influences. *Current Directions in Psychological Science*, 16(6): 300–304.

Belsky, J., & Pluess, M. (2009). Beyond diathesis stress: Differential susceptibility to environmental influences. *Psychological Bulletin*, 135(6): 885–908.

Berger, J. (1972). *Ways of Seeing*. London: Penguin.

Bernard, C. (1974) *Lectures on the phenomena common to animals and plants*. Trans: Hoff H.E. Springfield (IL): Charles C Thomas.

Bernfeld, S. D. (1944). Freud's earliest theories and the school of Helmholtz. *Psychoanalytic Quarterly*, 13: 341–362.

Bion, W. R. (1962). *Learning from Experience*. London: Heinemann.

Blass, R. B., & Carmeli, Z. (2007). The case against neuropsychoanalysis: On fallacies underlying psychoanalysis' latest scientific trend and its negative impact on psychoanalytic discourse. *International Journal of Psychoanalysis*, 88: 19–40.

Blass, R., & Carmeli, Z. (2015). Further evidence for the case against neuropsychoanalysis. *International Journal of Psychoanalysis*, 96: 1555–1573.

Bollas, C. (2019). The democratic state of mind. In: D. Morgan (Ed.), *The Unconscious in Social and Political Life* (pp. 27–38). London: Phoenix.

Botvinick, M. (2004). Probing the neural basis of body ownership. *Science*, 305: 782–783. doi: 10.1126/science.1101836

Boyce, W. (2019). *The Orchid and the Dandelion*. London: Pan Macmillan.

Brown, H., Adams, R., Parees, I., Edwards, M., & Friston, K. J. (2013). Active inference, sensory attenuation and illusions. *Cognitive Processing*, 14: 411–427. doi: 10.1007/s10339-013-0571-3

Budd, R., & Hughes, I. (2009). The Dodo Bird Verdict – controversial, inevitable and important: a commentary on 30 years of meta-analyses. *Clinical Psychology & Psychotherapy*, 16(6): 510–522. doi: 10.1002/cpp.648

Carhart-Harris, R. L., & Friston, K. J. (2010). The default mode, ego-functions and free energy: a neurobiological account of Freud's idea. *Brain*, 133: 1265–1283.

Carroll, L. (1871). *Through the Looking Glass and What Alice Found There*. Westport Eire: Everson, 2009.

Casement, P. (1981). *On Learning from the Patient*. London: Routledge.

Caspi, A., McClay, J., Moffitt, T. E., Mill, J., Martin, J., Craig, I. W., Taylor, A., & Poulton, R. (2002). Role of genotype in the cycle of violence in maltreated children. *Science*, 297: 851–854.

Clark, A. (2016). *Surfing Uncertainty*. Oxford: Oxford University Press.

Coan, J. (2016). Attachment and neuroscience. In: J. Cassidy & P. Shaver (Eds.), *Handbook of Attachment* (3rd edn.) (pp. 242–269). New York: Guilford Press.

Coan, J. A., Schaefer, H. S., & Davidson, R. J. (2006). Lending a hand: Social regulation of the neural response to threat. *Psychological Science*, 17(12): 1032–1039.

Coleridge, S. T. (1817). *Biographical Litereria*. J. Engell & W. Bate (Eds.). London: Routledge, 1983.

Colombo, M., & Wright, C. (2018). First principles in the life sciences, the free energy principle, organicism and mechanism. *Synthese:* 1–26.

Connolly, P. (2018). Expected free energy formalizes conflict underlying defence in Freudian psychoanalysis. *Frontiers in Psychology*. doi: 10.3389/psyg.2018.01264

Connolly, P., & van Deventer, V. (2017). Hierarchical recursive organisation and the free energy principle: from biological self-organisation to the psychoanalytic mind. *Frontiers in Psychology*. doi.org/190.3389/fpsyg.2017.01695

Constant, A., Ramstead, M., Veissiere, S., Campbell, J., & Friston,

K. J. (2018). A variational approach to niche construction. *Journal of the Royal Society Interface*, 15: 20170685. http://dx.doi.org/10.1098/rsif.2017.0685

Craig, T. K. J., Rus-Calafell, M., Ward, T., Leff, J. P., Huckvale, M., Emsley, R., Howarth, E., & Garety, P. A. (2017). AVATAR therapy for auditory verbal hallucinosis in people with psychosis: a single-blind randomised controlled trial. *Lancet Psychiatry*, 5(1): 31–40. doi: 10:1016/S2215-0366(17)30427-3

Csibra, G., & Gergely, G. (2009). Natural pedagogy. *Trends in Cognitive Sciences*, 13: 148–153.

Cunningham, W. A., & Brosch, T. (2012). Motivational salience: amygdala tuning from traits, needs, values, and goals. *Current Directions in Psychological Science*, 21: 54–59. doi: 10.1177/0963721411430832

Dayan, P., Hinton, G., Neal, R., & Zemel, R. (1995). The Helmholtz machine. *Neural Computation*, 7: 889–904.

Dennett, D. (2017). *From Bacteria to Bach and Back*. London: Allen Lane.

Devlin, K. (2003). Bayesian probability. *The Guardian* newspaper, March 20.

Dozier, M., Peloso, E., Lewis, E., Laurenceau, J., & Levine, S. (2008). Effects of an attachment-based intervention on the cortisol production of infants and toddlers in foster care. *Development and Psychopathology*, 20(3): 845–859.

Duquette, P., & Ainley, V. (2019). Working with the predictable life of patients: the importance of mentalised interoceptions to meaningful change in psychotherapy. *Frontiers in Psychology*, 26 September. https://doi.org/10.3389/fpsyg.2019.02173

Duschinsky, R. (2019). *Cornerstones: attachment in the 21st Century*. London: Routledge.

Eliot, T. S. (1962). *The Cocktail Party*. London: Faber.

Ermakova, A., Knolle, F., Justicia, A., Bullmore, E., Jones, P., Robbins, T., Fletcher, P., & Murray, G. (2018). Abnormal reward prediction error signalling in antipsychotic naïve individuals with first episode psychosis or clinical risk for first episode psychosis. *Neuropharmacology*, 43: 1691–1699.

Feldman, R. (2015a). Sensitive periods in human social development: New insights from research on oxytocin, synchrony, and high-risk parenting. *Development and Psychopathology*, 27: 369–395.

Feldman, R. (2015b). The adaptive human parental brain: Implications for children's social development. *Trends in Neuroscience*, 38: 387–399.

Fonagy, P., & Allison, E. (2014). The role of mentalizing and epistemic trust in the therapeutic relationship. *Psychotherapy*, 51(3): 372–380.

Fonagy, P., Gergely, G., Jurist, E., & Target, M. (2002). *Affect Regulation, Mentalization, and the Development of the Self.* New York: Other Press.

Fotopoulou, A., & Tsakiris, M. (2017). Mentalizing homeostasis: the social origins of interoceptive inference. *Neuropsychoanalysis*, 19: 3–28. doi:10:1080/152941145.2017.1294031

Freud, S. (1900a). *The Interpretation of Dreams. S. E., 4–5.* London: Hogarth.

Freud, S. (1911b). *Formulations on the two principles of mental functioning. S. E., 12.* London: Hogarth.

Freud, S. (1912b). *The dynamics of transference. S. E., 12.* London: Hogarth.

Freud, S. (1912–13). *Totem and Taboo. S. E., 13.* London: Hogarth.

Freud, S. (1916–17). *Introductory Lectures on Psycho-Analysis. S. E., 15–16.* London: Hogarth.

Freud, S. (1920g). *Beyond the Pleasure Principle. S. E., 18.* London: Hogarth.

Freud, S. (1924e). *The Loss of Reality in Neurosis and Psychosis. S. E., 19.* London: Hogarth.

Freud, S. (1925d). *An Autobiographical Study. S. E., 20.* London: Hogarth.

Freud, S. (1940a). *An Outline of Psycho-Analysis. S. E., 23.* London: Hogarth.

Freud, S. (1950a). *A Project for a Scientific Psychology. S. E., 1:* 95–397. London: Hogarth.

Freud, S., & Breuer, J. (1895d). *Studies on Hysteria. S. E.,2*. London: Hogarth.

Friston, K. J. (2010). The free energy principle: a unified brain theory? *Nature Reviews Neuroscience*, 11: 127–138.

Friston, K. J., Fortier, M., & Friedman, D. A. (2018). Of woodlice and men: A Bayesian account of cognition, life and consciousness. An interview with Karl Friston. *ALIUS Bulletin*, 2: 17–43.

Friston, K. J., & Frith, C. (2015). A duet for one. *Consciousness and Cognition*. https://doi.org/10.1016/j.concog.2014.12.003

Friston, K. J., Thornton, C., & Clark, A. (2012). Free energy minimisation and the dark-room problem. *Frontiers in Psychology*, 3: 1–7. doi: 10.3389/fpsyg.2012.00130

Frith, C. (2012). The role of metacognition in human social interactions. *Philosophical Transactions of the Royal Society B*. doi: 10.1098/rstb2012.0123

Gabbard, G., & Ogden, T (2009). On becoming a psychoanalyst. *International Journal of Psychoanalysis*, 90: 311–327.

Garland, C. (Ed.) (2002). *Understanding Trauma: a Psychoanalytic Approach* (2nd edn.). London: Routledge.

Gibson, J. (1986). *The Ecological Approach to Visual Perception*. Hillsdale, NJ: Lawrence Erlbaum Associates.

Ginot, E. (2015). *The Neuropsychology of the Unconscious*. New York: W. W. Norton.

Gombrich, E. (1960). *Art and Illusion*. London: Phaedon.

Graziano, M. (2019). Attributing awareness to others: The attention schema theory and its relationship to behavioral prediction. *Journal of Consciousness Studies*, 26(3–4): 17–37.

Gu, X., Hof, P. R., Friston, K. J., & Fan, J. (2013). Anterior insular cortex and emotional awareness. *Journal of Comparative Neurology*, 521: 3371–3388. http://dx.doi.org/10.1002/cne.23368

Harrison, K. (2013). *The 5:2 Diet Book*. London: Orion.

Hobson, J. A., & Friston, K. J. (2012). Waking and dreaming

consciousness: neurobiological and functional considerations. *Progress in Neurobiology*, 98: 82–98.

Hobson, J. A., Hong, C. C., & Friston, K. J. (2014). Virtual reality and consciousness inference in dreaming. *Frontiers in Psychology / Cognitive Science*, 5: 1133. doi: 10.3389/fpsyg.2014.01133

Hofer, M. (2002). Clinical implications drawn from the new biology of attachment. *Journal of Infant, Child & Adolescent Psychotherapy*, 2(4):157–162.

Hohwy, J. (2013). *The Predictive Mind*. Oxford: Oxford University Press.

Holler, J., Kendrick, K., Casillas, M., & Levinson, S. D. (2015). Turn-taking in human communicative interaction. *Frontiers in Psychology*. doi: 10.3389/fpsyg.2015.01919

Holmes, J. (2010). *Exploring in Security: towards an Attachment-informed Psychotherapy*. London: Routledge.

Holmes, J. (2013). *John Bowlby and Attachment Theory* (2nd edn.). London: Routledge.

Holmes, J. (2014). *The Therapeutic Imagination: Using Literature to Deepen Psychodynamic Understanding and Enhanced Empathy*. London: Routledge.

Holmes J., & Bateman, A. (Eds.) (2002). *Psychotherapy Integration*. London: Routledge.

Holmes, J., & Nolte, T. (2019). Surprise and the Bayesean brain: implications for psychotherapy theory and practice. *Frontiers in Psychology*. doi: 10.3389/fpsyg.2019.00592

Holmes, J., & Slade, A. S. (2017). *Attachment in Therapeutic Practice*. London: SAGE.

Holmes, J., & Slade, A. S. (2019). The neuroscience of attachment: implications for psychological therapies. *British Journal of Psychiatry*, 214: 318–320.

Holmes, R. (1989). *Coleridge: Early Visions*. London: Hodder & Stoughton.

Holt, R. (1962). A critical examination of Freud's concept of bound vs free cathexis. *Psychoanalytic Quarterly*, 32: 446–452.

Hopkins, J. (2016). Free energy and virtual reality in neuroscience and psychoanalysis: a complexity theory of dreaming and mental disturbance. *Frontiers in Psychology.* https://doi.org/10.3389/fpsyg.2016.00922

Hopson, J. (2019). Stigma and fear: the psy-professional in cultural artefacts. *British Journal of Psychotherapy*, 35: 233–244.

Humphrey, N. (2011). *Soul Dust.* Princeton, NY: Princeton University Press.

James, W. (1890). *The Principles of Psychology.* New York: Dover, 1950.

Joffily, M., & Coricelli, G. (2013). Emotional valence and the free-energy principle. *PLOS Computational Biology*, 9(6): e1003094.

Kahneman, J. (2011). *Thinking: Fast and Slow.* London: Allen Lane.

Kandel, E. (2012). *The Age of Insight: The Quest to Understand the Unconscious in Art, Mind, and Brain, from Vienna 1900 to the Present.* New York: Random House.

Kashdan, T., Barrett, L., & McKnight, P. (2015). Unpacking emotion differentiation: transforming unpleasant experience by perceiving distinctions in negativity. *Current Directions in Psychological Science*, 24(1): 10–16. https://doi.org/10.1177/0963721414550708

Kidd, C., Piantadosi, S., & Aslin, R. (2012). The Goldilocks effect: human infants allocate attention to visual sequences that are neither too simple nor too complex. *PLOS One*, 7(50): e363999. doi: 10.1371/journal.pone.0036399

Kim, D., Wampold, B., & Bolt, D. (2004). Therapist effects in psychotherapy: A random-effects modeling of the National Institute of Mental Health Treatment of Depression Collaborative Research Program data. *Psychotherapy Research*, 16: 161–172.

Kirchhoff, M. (2017). Predictive brains and embodied enactive cognition: an introduction to special issue. *Synthese*, 195(6): 2355–2366.

Kirchhoff, M., Parr, T., Palacios, E., Friston, K. J., & Kiverstein, J. (2018). The Markov blankets of life: autonomy, active inference and the free energy principle. *Journal of the Royal Society Interface*, 15: e20170792. doi:10.1098/rsif.2017.0792

Knox, J. (2010). *Self-agency in Psychotherapy*. New York: W. W. Norton.

Kris, E. (1952). *Psychoanalytic Explorations in Art*. New York: International Universities Press.

Kyselo, M. (2014). The body social: an enactive approach to the self. *Frontiers in Psychology*, 5: 1–16.

Lambert, M. (2013). Outcome in psychotherapy: the past and important advances. *Psychotherapy*, 50: 42–51.

Lanius, R. A., Frewen, P. A., Tursich, M., Jetly, R., & McKinnon, M. C. (2015). Restoring large-scale brain networks in PTSD and related disorders: A proposal for neuroscientifically informed treatment interventions. *European Journal of Psychotraumatology*, 6.

Laplanche, J. (1987). *New Foundations for Psychoanalysis*. D. Macey (Trans.). Oxford: Blackwell.

Laplanche, J. (2009). Transference: its provocation by the analyst. In: J. Birkstead-Breen, S. Flanders, & A. Gibeault (Eds.), J. Cheshire (Trans.), *Reading French Psychoanalysis*. London: Routledge.

Laplanche, J., & Pontalis, J. (1973). *The Language of Psychoanalysis*. D. Nicholson-Smith (Trans.). London: Hogarth.

Lear, J. (2011). *A Case for Irony*. Cambridge, MA: Harvard University Press.

Leichsenring, F. (2008). Effectiveness of long-term psychodynamic psychotherapy. *Journal of the American Medical Association*, 300: 1551–1565.

Lemma, A., Target, M., & Fonagy, P. (2008). *Brief Dynamic Interpersonal Therapy: a Clinician's Guide*. Oxford: Oxford University Press.

Litowitz, B. (2014). From switch-words to stitch words. *International Journal of Psychoanalysis*, 95: 3–14.

Loewald, H. (1960). On the therapeutic action of psychoanalysis. *International Journal of Psychoanalysis*, 41: 16–33.

Maier, S. F., & Seligman, M. E. (2016). Learned helplessness at fifty: Insights from neuroscience. *Psychological Review*, 123: 349–367.

Masterpaqua, F., & Perna, P. A. (Eds.) (1997). *The Psychological Meaning of chaos: Translating Theory into Practice*. Washington, DC: American Psychological Association.

Meares, R. (2005). *The Metaphor of Play* (3rd edn.). London: Routledge.

Meins, E., Fernyhough, C., Fradley, E., & Tuckey, M. (2001). Re-thinking maternal sensitivity: Mothers' comments in infants' mental processes predict security of attachment at 12 months. *Journal of Child Psychology and Psychiatry*, 42(5): 637–648.

Mellor, M. (2018). Making worlds in a waking dream: where Bion intersects Friston on the shaping and breaking of psychic reality. *Frontiers in Psychology*, 9. 10.3389/fpsyg.201801674.

Mikulincer, N., & Shaver, P. (2007). *Attachment in Adulthood*. New York: Guilford Press.

Moutoussis, M., Shahar, N., Hauser, T. U., & Dolan, R. J. (2018). Computation in psychotherapy, or how computational psychiatry can aid learning-based psychological therapies. *Computers in Psychiatry*, 2: 50–73. doi: 10.1162/CPSY_a_00014

Nagel, T. (1974). What is it like to be a bat? *Philosophical Review*, 83(4): 435–450.

Northoff, G. (2012). From emotions to consciousness – a neuro-phenomenal and neuro-relational account. *Frontiers in Psychology*. doi: 10.3389/fpsyg.2012.00303

Northoff, G., & Panksepp, J. (2008). The trans-species concept of self and the subcortical mid-line system. *Trends in Cognitive Science*, 12: 259–264.

Ogden, T (1994) The Analytic Third: Working with Intersubjective Clinical Facts. *International Journal of Psychoanalysis* 75: 3-19

Ongaro, G., & Kaptchuk, T. (2018). Symptom perception, placebo effects and the Bayesean brain. *Pain*, 1–4. doi: 10.1097/j. pain.0000000000001367

Panksepp, J., & Solms, M. (2012). What is neuropsychoanalysis? Clinically relevant studies of the minded brain. *Trends in Cognitive Science*, 16: 6–8.

Parr, T., & Friston, K. J. (2018). The anatomy of inference: Generative models and brain structure. *Frontiers in Computational Neuroscience*. doi.org/10.3389/fncom.2018.00090

Pinker, S. (2003). *The Blank Slate*. London: Allen Lane.

Prigogine, L. (1980). *From Being to Becoming: Time and Complexity in the Physical Sciences*. New York: Freedman.

Putnam, K., Harris, W., & Putnam, F. (2013). Synergistic childhood adversities and complex adult psychopathology. *Journal of Traumatic Stress*, 26: 435–442.

Ramstead, M. J., Badcock, P. B., & Friston, K. J. (2017). Answering Schrödinger's question: A free-energy formulation. *Physics of Life Reviews*. https://doi.org/10.1016/j.plrev.2017.09.001

Ramstead, M. J., Veissiere, S. P., & Kirmayer, L. J. (2016). Cultural affordances: Scaffolding local worlds through shared intentionality and regimes of attention. *Frontiers in Psychology*, 7: 1090.

Rovelli, C. (2017). *Reality Is Not What It Seems*. London: Allen Lane.

Rutter, M. (2012). Resilience as a dynamic concept. *Development and Psychopathology*, 24: 335–344.

Safran, J. D. (2012). *Psychoanalysis and Psychoanalytic Therapies*. Washington, DC: American Psychological Association.

Saxbe, D., & Repetti, R. (2010). For better or worse? Coregulation of couples' cortisol levels and mood states. *Journal of Personality & Social Psychology*, 98: 92–103.

Schore, A. (2019). *The Development of the Unconscious Mind*. New York: W. W. Norton.

Schroedinger, E. (1944). *What Is Life? The Physical Aspect of the Living Cell*. Cambridge: Cambridge University Press.

References

Seth, A. (2013). Interoceptive inference, emotion, and the embodied self. *Trends in Cognitive Sciences*, 17: 565–673. doi: 10.1016/j.tics.2013.09.007

Shedler, J. (2010). The efficacy of psychodynamic psychotherapy. *American Psychologist*, 65: 98–109.

Smith, R., Lane, R., Nadel, L., & Moutoussis, M. (2019a). A computational neuroscience perspective on the change process in psychotherapy. In: R. Lane & L. Nadel (Eds.), *Neuroscience of Enduring Change: Implications for Psychotherapy*. Oxford: Oxford University Press.

Smith, R., Lane, R., Parr, T., & Friston, K. J. (2019b). Neurocomputational mechanisms underlying emotional awareness: insights afforded by deep active inference and their potential relevance. *Neuroscience and Biobehavioural Reviews*. doi. org/10.1101/681288

Solms, M. (2019). The hard problem of consciousness and the free energy principle. *Frontiers in Psychology*, 9. doi: 10.3389/fpsyg.2018.02714

Strachey, J. (1934). The nature of the therapeutic action of psycho-analysis. *International Journal of Psychoanalysis*, 15: 126–159.

Suomi, S. (2016). Attachment in rhesus monkeys. In: J. Cassidy & P. Shaver (Eds.), *Handbook of Attachment* (3rd edn.) (pp. 133–154). New York: Guilford Press.

Talia, A., Daniel, S. I., Miller-Bottome, M., Brambilla, D., Miccoli, D., Safran, J. D., & Lingiardi, V. (2014). AAI predicts patients' in-session interpersonal behavior and discourse: a "move to the level of the relation" for attachment-informed psychotherapy research. *Attachment & Human Development*, 16: 192–209. doi:10.1080/14616734.2013.859161

Talia, A., Muzi, L., Lingiardi, V., & Taubner, S. (2018). How to be a secure base: therapists' attachment representations and their link to attunement in psychotherapy. *Attachment & Human Development*, 20: 1–18.

Talia, A., Taubner, S., & Miller-Bottome, M. (2019). Advances in research on attachment-related psychotherapy processes: Seven teaching points for trainees and supervisors. *Research in Psychotherapy: Psychopathology, Process and Outcome*, 22(3).

Target, M. (2007). Is our sexuality our own? An attachment model of sexuality based on early affect mirroring. *British Journal of Psychotherapy*, 23: 517–530.

Taylor, D. (2015). Pragmatic randomized controlled trial of long-term psychoanalytic psychotherapy for treatment resistant depression: The Tavistock Adult Depression Study (TADS). *World Psychiatry*, 14: 312–321.

Tomasello, M. (2018) *Becoming Human: A Theory of Ontogeny*. Cambridge, (Mass): Belknap Press.

Tottenham, N. (2014). The importance of early experiences for neuro-affective development. In: S. Anderson & D. Pine (Eds.), *The Neurobiology of Childhood* (Vol. 16) (pp. 109–129). Berlin: Springer.

Tozzi, A., & Peters, J. (2017). Critique of free energy principle. *Physics of Life Reviews*. doi: 10.1016/j.plrev.2017.10.003

Van Os, J. (2009). Salience dysregulation syndrome. *British Journal of Psychiatry*, 194: 101–103.

Vrticka, P. (2016). The social neuroscience of attachment. In: A. Ibáñez, L. Sedeño, & A. M. García (Eds.), *Neuroscience and Social Science* (pp. 95-119). Cham, Switzerland: Springer. doi 10.1007/978-3-319-68421-5_5

Wampold, B. (2015). How important are the common factors in psychotherapy? An update. *World Psychiatry*, 14: 270–277.

Weng, H., Lapate, R., Stodola, D., Rogers, G., & Davidson, R. (2018). Visual attention to suffering after compassion training is associated with decreased amygdala responses. *Frontiers in Psychology*. doi.org/10.3389/fpsyg.2018.00771

Wilson, D. (2002). *Darwin's Cathedral*. Chigago, IL: University of Chicago Press.

Wilson, D., & Sperber, D. (2002). Truthfulness and relevance.

Mind, 111(443): 583–632.

Winnicott, D. W. (1960). The theory of the parent-infant relation-ship. *International Journal of Psychoanalysis*, 41: 585–595.

Winnicott, D. W. (1965). *The Maturational Processes and the Facili-tating Environment*. London: Hogarth.

Yalom, I. (2011). *Staring at the Sun*. New York: Basic Books.

Yon, D., de Lange, F. P., & Press, C. (2019). The predictive brain as a stubborn scientist. *Trends in Cognitive Sciences*, 23(1): 6–8.

Yovell, Y., Solms, M., & Fotopoulou, A. (2015). The case for neuropsychoanalysis: Why a dialogue with neuroscience is necessary but not sufficient for psychoanalysis. *International Journal of Psychoanalysis*, 96: 1515–1553.

INDEX

Index